American Schools

The Art of Creating a Democratic Learning Community

Sam Chaltain

ROWMAN & LITTLEFIELD EDUCATION
A division of
ROWMAN & LITTLEFIELD PUBLISHERS, INC.
Lanham • New York • Toronto • Plymouth, UK

Published by Rowman & Littlefield Education
A division of Rowman & Littlefield Publishers, Inc.
A wholly owned subsidary of The Rowman & Littlefield Publishing Group, Inc.
4501 Forbes Boulevard, Suite 200, Lanham, Maryland 20706
http://www.rowmaneducation.com

Estover Road, Plymouth PL6 7PY, United Kingdom

British Library Cataloguing in Publication Information Available

Library of Congress Cataloging-in-Publication Data

Chaltain, Sam.
  American schools : the art of creating a democratic learning community / Sam Chaltain.
    p. cm.
  Includes bibliographical references.
  ISBN 978-1-60709-253-7 (cloth : alk. paper) — ISBN 978-1-60709-255-1 (electronic)
  1. Educational leadership—United States—History—21st century. 2. School administration—United States—History—21st century. 3. Schools—United States—History—21st century. I. Title.
  LB2805.C427 2010
  371.200973—dc22   2009022689

∞™ The paper used in this publication meets the minimum requirements of American National Standard for Information Sciences—Permanence of Paper for Printed Library Materials, ANSI/NISO Z39.48-1992. Printed in the United States of America

We the People of the United States, in Order to form a more perfect Union, establish Justice, insure domestic Tranquility, provide for the common defence, promote the general Welfare, and secure the Blessings of Liberty to ourselves and our Posterity, do ordain and establish this Constitution for the United States of America.

—Preamble, United States Constitution

Congress shall make no law respecting an establishment of religion, or prohibiting the free exercise thereof; or abridging the freedom of speech, or of the press; or the right of the people peaceably to assemble, and to petition the Government for a redress of grievances.

—First Amendment, United States Constitution

Only the educated are free.

—Epictetus

For Vic

Contents

About the Images

The images on the cover and in the prologue and chapters 1–5 come from *Amherst College: Building Community Through Learning Project* (2006–2008), a community art project facilitated by artists Wendy Ewald and Brett Cook.

A multifaceted process that included the collaborative development of eighteen large-scale portraits made by students, faculty, and staff, the Amherst project culminated with the public mounting of the works across the college community and an exhibition at the Mead Art Museum. A full set of images and narrative about the project can be found in *Who Am I in This Picture: Amherst Community Portraits* (Amherst College Press, 2009). To learn more about the Amherst collaborative art project, visit http://www3.amherst.edu/~ccsp11/collaborative_art/.

To learn more about Brett Cook, a creative person who engages in individual and collaborative processes of expression to promote community, and to celebrate the interconnectedness of all things, visit www.brett-cook.com.

To learn more about Wendy Ewald, an artist who has collaborated with children and adults around the world for forty years, encouraging them to use cameras to create self-portraits and to articulate their fantasies and dreams, visit www.wendyewald.com.

The images at the beginning of chapters 6–8 and the epilogue were taken by the author.

The photographs in chapter 8 were taken by Cassandra Carland, the student whose story is featured in that chapter. To see more of Cass's images, visit http://www.flickr.com/photos/smugglerkiss.

Foreword

Sandra Day O'Connor

Every year, on September 17 (Constitution Day), schoolchildren across the country learn about a hot summer in 1787 when a special generation of men gathered in Philadelphia to create a new nation.

This nationwide process of remembering our past is an important step. Constitution Day also affords us an opportunity to reflect on a core question for the future: the extent to which our schools remain committed to the mission that was the reason for their founding.

As we all know, a healthy democracy demands sustained participation from each new generation. To help encourage that participation, we have our public education system—the only institution in the United States that engages 90 percent of the next generation of adults, is governed by public authority, and has the explicit mission to prepare people for the rights and responsibilities of democratic citizenship.

Despite this clear mandate, civic education—and, with it, civic learning—has been in steady decline for decades. As a result, too many young people today do not understand how our political system works, or how to be seen and heard in meaningful, effective ways.

I joined former congressman Lee Hamilton to cochair the Campaign for the Civic Mission of Schools (www.civicmissionofschools.org) because I am disturbed by the following facts: Only one-third of Americans can name the three branches of government. Two-thirds know at least one of the judges on *American Idol*. Less than one in one hundred can identify the chief justice of the United States. And the average American is more likely to know the five members of the Simpsons cartoon family than the five freedoms of the First Amendment.

This last fact is particularly disturbing, since the First Amendment's five freedoms are our chief tools for sharing our voices and making our opinions known in a democracy. Researchers from the University of Connecticut, funded by the John S. and James L. Knight Foundation, have been collecting data for years "to determine whether relationships exist—and, if so, the nature of those relationships—between what teachers and administrators think, and what students . . . know about the First Amendment."

As the 2007 report on "The Future of the First Amendment" (www.firstamendmentfuture.org) makes clear, the news is discouraging. "It appears," the researchers write, "that our nation's high schools are failing their students when it comes to instilling in them an appreciation for the First Amendment." Among their findings:

- Students lack knowledge and understanding about the First Amendment. Nearly three-fourths say they don't know how they feel about it or that they take it for granted.
- Just 8 percent of teachers say their school has made "a lot" of effort to promote First Amendment principles through school activities, conversations, and policies.
- Perhaps most disturbing, one out of every three American high school students thinks the First Amendment goes too far in the rights it guarantees.

The Knight Foundation's study provides an important wakeup call for anyone who cares about the future of American democracy. I share Sam Chaltain's belief that schools must play an essential role in answering that call, by preparing America's young people to be active, engaged citizens.

The bad news is that in recent years schools have narrowed their curricula to try and reach the ambitious math and reading standards established by the No Child Left Behind (NCLB) Act of 2001. At least half of the states no longer make the teaching of civics and government a requirement for high school graduation.

The promise of NCLB has been its focus on achievement and its insistence that all students have a right to highly qualified teachers. But as the Forum for Education and Democracy explains in its 2008 report, *Democracy at Risk*, "The law has not provided the resources to achieve these goals, and it has not focused on the kind of higher-order thinking and performance skills needed in the 21st century. These include the abilities required by social and democratic life to apply knowledge to complex, novel problems, communicate and collaborate effectively, and find, manage, and analyze information."

Ensuring that young people acquire the skills democracy imposes on us will require a concerted effort in school districts, at statehouses, and by the federal government. The pending congressional reauthorization of NCLB and the inauguration of our forty-fourth president make this an ideal time for *American Schools* to arrive, and for us all to remember that the primary purpose of public schools in America has been to help produce citizens who have the knowledge, the skills, and the values needed to sustain our centuries-old experiment in liberty.

As Sam Chaltain makes clear in the pages that follow, we can't expect our schools to become more democratic if our school leaders don't understand how to create more equitable school environments. And we can't expect our democracy to perform well if students do not learn about basic concepts of government or receive meaningful opportunities to exercise their rights responsibly.

Knowledge about our government is not handed down through the gene pool. Every generation has to learn it, and we all learn best by *doing*.

The good news is that research clearly shows how civic learning contributes to a healthy and high-functioning school environment. Schools that pay attention to civic learning are more likely to help young people build strong character and develop the attitudes and relationships that are essential for success in the twenty-first century workplace and society. Students who participate in classroom discussions about current issues have a greater interest in politics, improved critical thinking and communication skills, more civic knowledge, and greater interest in discussing public affairs outside of school.

To help educators create these sorts of conditions, Sam has pioneered a new approach to school leadership. And to help teachers create these sorts of learning opportunities, I've had the privilege of working with others to pioneer a new teaching method.

Our Courts (www.ourcourts.org) is a free, interactive, Web-based program designed to supply the next generation with the tools they will need for informed civic engagement and leadership. Through the lens of the judiciary, Our Courts allows students to participate in realistic simulations of government and to grapple with relevant social issues. They can investigate and argue actual cases and controversies using real law, and they can view these cases from the perspective of the judicial, legislative, and executive branches of government. Our Courts also encourages young people to act, by voicing their opinions in their communities and to their elected representatives.

We have important work to do. Public education is a vitally important solution to preserving an independent judiciary and maintaining a robust constitutional democracy. The better educated our young people are, the better equipped they will be to preserve the system of government we have. And for each student who is educated in intellectually engaging ways, we will gain the greatest strength a democratic society must have: an informed and engaged citizen able to think freely and independently and contribute to society as a whole.

Washington, D.C.
April 2009

Acknowledgments

This book interweaves a decade's worth of conversations, reflections, frustrations, and insights. I am grateful to everyone who was a part of that journey.

I am particularly indebted to the school leaders whose stories are featured in part II. By allowing the rest of us to learn from their professional and personal journeys, Rob Williams, Mary Kennerly, and Kim Carter model the type of courage and transparency to which we should all aspire.

When it was time to take a pile of observations and try to turn them into comprehensible stories, Kenny Holdsman, Jeremy Zucker, Sharon Robinson, George Wood, Denise Borders, Andrea Cahn, Molly McCloskey, Terry Roberts, Carl Glickman, John Goodlad, Aileen Chaltain, and Reg Gibbons provided thoughtful feedback, suggested new paths to pursue, and pushed me to be ever clearer. My friends from the League of Democratic Schools provided a final round of useful feedback on the prologue, especially Rona Wilensky. Terry Pickeral and Ted McConnell helped open my eyes to new possibilities. Ron Collins schooled me on the business of sharing ideas. Bill McIntyre and Susan Oliver uncovered the book's core messages for me. Todd Nocera and Brett Cook helped make the words visible. The great people at Rowman & Littlefield—particularly Patti Belcher, Elaine McGarraugh, and Sam Caggiula—produced a book that I can feel proud to show my grandmother. And Knox Johnstone and Cornelia Spelman get extra credit, since, as my biological parents, they are more responsible for this book's creation than anyone else.

To the First Amendment Center's Charles Haynes and the Knight Foundation's Alberto Ibarguen, I owe the highest debt of gratitude. Since I met him in 2000, Charles has been a friend, mentor, and source of inspiration whose trail I am honored to follow. And without Alberto's faith in me, I would not have had the self-confidence, freedom, and support I needed to put these thoughts to paper.

Finally, to Sarah—fellow traveler, sounding board, perspective provider, and most constant source of editorial advice, insight, and inspiration. Here's to all the journeys still to come.

Introduction

Ask different people to define what it means to be an American in a single word, and you'll hear the same answer—FREEDOM.

In that one word we capture the historic, partly fulfilled promise of the United States. And we name an irresistible, universal human impulse—to be in control of our own destiny, to feel visible to others, and to have a say in determining the shape of the world around us.

Alongside the need for freedom, there is an equally pressing human desire—for structure, safety, and a sense of order to the world.

These two universal needs—for freedom on one hand and structure on the other—are particularly relevant to our nation's school leaders, who must strike the right balance between the two in order to create healthy, high-functioning learning environments.

In my years as an educator, I have witnessed scores of schools that choose, consciously or unconsciously, to value one of these needs at the expense of the other. I wrote this book to deliver a message to school leaders: *You do not need to choose*. It is possible—indeed, essential—to find the right organizational balance between individual freedom and group structure. In fact, research confirms that when school leaders do so, they create optimal conditions for student learning, motivation, and engagement.

Now, more than ever, our country needs these sorts of schools. We need schools that provide young people with well-structured spaces in which to discover who they are and what they care deeply about. We need schools where adults prepare students for active citizenship and the twenty-first-century workplace. And we need schools to reinforce democratic practices that extend beyond the school's walls, helping adults unite behind the shared belief that all children deserve to be seen and heard.

Before that vision can become a reality, we must ensure that the central elements of our social covenant are also in place in our schools: a clear sense of structure and shared identity on one hand, and an unwavering commitment to individual freedom on the other.

American Schools will help school leaders achieve this important goal. Part I, *Theory*, outlines an actionable five-part framework for leadership, grounded in democratic principles ("principles for principals"), and it identifies the essential skills educators must cultivate in themselves and in others to create the conditions that best support more equitable, engaging, relationship-driven learning environments. Part II, *Practice*, provides an opportunity for readers to apply what they learned in part I by way of the stories of three school communities that have, over several years, tried to create model democratic learning communities—to differing degrees of success.

Fred Givens, the middle school principal of Bronx Prep Charter School in New York City, knows what it feels like when this delicate balance is achieved. Asked to reflect on his school's ongoing work to value individual freedoms and create an orderly environment that improves student learning, Givens observed: "Some of us have learned that—despite what intuition might suggest—structure actually creates freedom. Through experiences implementing democratic principles in the classroom and in the process of co-creating our shared culture, it has become clear that the potential for looseness, play, free thought, and creativity is generated when the structures are so tight and elegantly constructed that they become nearly invisible. This has been a fundamental revelation."

All of us—whether we are students, parents, supporters, teachers, or administrators—must become more attuned to these "degrees of freedom" and to the individual and group needs of the people around us. When we do so, we create the types of schools that confer not just academic diplomas, but also "degrees" of individual freedom, of civic responsibility, and of shared respect for the power and uniqueness of each person's voice.

I hope you enjoy the book.

Prologue
Ways of Seeing (and of Being Seen): The Art of the Democratic Learning Community

From 165 photos of Amherst College faculty, students, and staff, artists Wendy Ewald and Brett Cook chose nine to transform into large mural prints and nine into original ink drawings that would form the basis of collaborative murals.

"Sawa Bona." (A common greeting among tribes in northern Natal in South Africa. Literally translated, it means, "I see you.")

"Sikhona." (The traditional response, which means, "I am here.")

My first teaching experience, in the winter of 1994, was at a public university in Beijing, China.

Hired to teach third-year English majors an American literature course, I was twenty-two and had just graduated from college myself. In the weeks leading up to the class, I grew a beard to create the illusion of a greater distance between my age and theirs. I learned later it didn't work.

The night before my first class, I had a series of anxiety dreams. In one version I overslept my morning class, only to have my new bosses wake me by loudly knocking on the door of my dorm room. In another I was delivering a lesson when, halfway through, I realized I wasn't wearing pants. By the time I did wake up, I felt as though I'd been teaching for hours.

Trimming my beard, combing my hair, and putting on my most professional-looking clothes, I gathered my materials and took the short walk across campus to room 112. It was a cold February morning. A small group of elderly men and women practiced tai chi in a patch of snow-covered grass along the path. The smell of coal hung, omnipresent, in the gray air. Smokey wisps of breath escaped my lips as I struggled to slow my breathing to a manageable rhythm. There is nothing quite like those twin feelings of exhilaration and terror that accompany the moments before one's inaugural solo act as a teacher.

As I reached the door, I heard a few muffled voices happily chatting on the other side. The students at my university were from hometowns all over China; many of them were seeing their friends for the first time in two months. To try and add to the spirit of collegiality, I opened the door, concealed my nerves, and issued a hearty and friendly, "Good Morning!"

The room fell silent. I scanned thirty sets of eyes for some sort of reaction and found nothing. My students were all advanced in English, so much so that the university wanted them to take a subject course with a native speaker. But as the awkwardness grew while I led them through the syllabus, the silence growing ever louder—and longer—in my mind, I started to wonder if I'd entered the wrong room.

After about ten minutes, I turned my back to the class for the first time to write my name on the board. As I did, my silent students let out a loud and collective, "Ooooooh!"

I turned back toward the group—the memories of one particular dream still fresh in my mind. They giggled in unison, nervously. This is odd, I thought, but at least we're communicating. "What's so funny?" I asked, smiling. A lone hand came up at the back of the class.

"Yes?"

"Excuse us," she began, in halting English, "but in China, we believe that people who are left-handed are extremely intelligent."

"I see," I said. "In America, we also believe that to be true."

As the first day of classes wound down, I started to feel more relaxed and confident. Then I learned that in each of my classes, one student, who was to remain anonymous to me, had been assigned to the class because she was a member of the Communist Party. Her task? To ensure that classroom conversations with an American instructor always stayed within "acceptable guidelines."

It's worth noting that, not long after the semester began, these "anonymous" students introduced themselves to me during office hours, where we respectfully debated the pros and cons of our different societies. Yet the message about the kind of atmosphere the university wanted to establish, and the types of citizens it hoped to graduate, was clear.

As I thought about this, it made sense. In Chinese culture, the needs of the community are valued more than the interests of the individual, and the government believes that maintaining centralized control is a paramount societal concern. In that sense, my university was doing what it was supposed to do; it was reflecting the prevailing notions of what defined the ideal Chinese citizen.

⁂

During my last teaching experience, at a large public high school in Manhattan, the impulse toward censorship was subtler.

The building was a large, industrial-style rectangle of rooms and hallways. The school served 3,500 kids, reflecting the diversity of the city. In one class, a third of my thirty-five students interacted with me every day in their second or third language.

In part because of this diversity, my school leaders believed the best way to ensure a safe learning environment was by maintaining a firm sense of control. I learned this inadvertently one day, about four weeks into my teaching, during the first fire drill of the year.

Although I had never been briefed on the protocol, my students knew exactly what to do when the alarm went off. All of them stood up and moved to the right of their desks, silently awaiting instructions. "OK," I guessed, "let's go outside."

As I entered the concrete hallways, I looked in both directions to see what other classrooms were doing. What I saw were long lines of students, silently awaiting further instructions.

Some educators might feel I've just described their organizational fantasy. In the weeks and months that followed, however, I witnessed other ways in which this emphasis on control had stunted the ability of my students to make thoughtful, informed decisions about themselves and their classmates. Some had never been asked to form an opinion about the material they were studying. Most had never been asked to demonstrate their understanding of what they learned in any other way than a standardized, multiple-choice test. The expectations were to follow directions and memorize the information we gave them—not to inquire about the nature of knowledge, themselves, or their place in the world.

I believe this culture exacted a heavy cost. Indeed, whereas in China it was the government silencing young people's voices, here in America, where we believe all human beings are born with certain inalienable rights, it is our own educational system inhibiting the capacity of young people to learn how to use their voices effectively. What results is the perpetuation of a familiar expression—*children are to be seen, not heard.*

THE DESIRE TO BE VISIBLE

Today, too many schools are still structured to reflect an Industrial-age philosophy about the proper management of human beings. As Stanford professor Linda Darling-Hammond explains in her book *The Right to Learn*, "Although schools have changed some in the last one hundred years, most are still organized to impart a largely fact-based, rote-oriented curriculum through structures that do not allow long-term teacher-student relationships or in-depth study.

"Over and over again," Darling-Hammond writes, "research and casual observation reveal that in most bureaucratically organized schools, students feel alienated from teachers, who appear to have little time for students unless they are unusually 'bright' or 'problematic.' Teachers feel at odds with administrators, who appear to have little time for them unless their concerns pertain to contractual matters, mandates, or paperwork. And everyone feels victimized by the 'system,' which demands attention to reports and procedures when teachers, students, and administrators would rather devote their time to each other and to learning."[1]

This approach is no longer tenable. When we as leaders do not trust, believe in, or have opportunities to recognize the true worth and potential of the fellow human beings we are supposed to serve, we manage each other as we would manage inanimate things.

What develops is a vicious cycle. As organizational consultant Stephen Covey has written, "This widespread reluctance to take initiative, to act independently, only fuels formal leaders' imperative to direct or manage their subordinates. This, they believe, is what they must do in order to get followers to act. . . . Each party's weakness reinforces and ultimately justifies the other's behavior." The more a principal or a teacher controls, Covey explains, "the more s/he evokes behaviors that necessitate greater control or managing. The co-dependent culture that develops is eventually institutionalized to the point that no one takes responsibility."[2]

All of us have likely experienced this sort of culture at some point in our careers. It is always undesirable. But the stakes are much greater when this sort of dynamic characterizes a school.

I realized this several years ago when, while sharing a meal with a friend who was a journalist, the conversation turned to the American educational system. "If there were only one thing you'd want our public schools to achieve," he asked me, "what would it be?"

I had not thought of the question so narrowly before. The prompt helped me realize that if there is only one thing I would want schools to guarantee, it would be to help all young people acquire the skills and self-confidence they need to be visible in the world.

As every educator knows, there is in each of us a deep, powerful, and fundamental need to be seen and heard. We want to discover our own voice—and learn how to use it effectively. Biology professor James Zull, the director of Case Western University's Center for Innovation in Teaching and Education and the author of *The Art of Changing the Brain*, speaks of this impulse to participate in biological terms, describing it as the irrepressible "urge to speak."[3] And Myles Horton, the founder of the Highlander adult education schools that helped train activists like Rosa Parks, believes democratic practices are the ideal frame through which our many different voices can be heard. "I think it's important to understand that the quality of the process you use to get to a place determines the ends, so when you want to build a democratic society, you have to act democratically in every way. . . . When you believe in a democratic society, you must provide a setting for education that is democratic."[4]

In a democracy (or a school), our voice is the chief tool we have to satisfy this basic human desire to be seen and heard by others. Learning how to use language effectively is therefore one of our chief resources for becoming visible to the world.

This is not some abstract idea of elevated prose—it is the act of helping unlock the mystery of ourselves through the discovery of the right words to explain who we are, what we need, and what we believe. As the poet Alan Grossman puts it, it is "making persons present to one another in that special sense in which they are acknowledgeable and therefore capable of love and mutual interest in one another's safety."[5] And as biologist and neuroscientist Francisco Varela explains, "We can only see what we can talk about, because we are speaking 'blind,' beyond language. Language is like another set of eyes and hands for the nervous system, through which we coordinate actions with others. We exist in language. It is by languaging and recurrent actions or human practices that we create meaning together. This is what I call the enactive view of knowing the world; we lay it down as we walk on its path."[6]

When we learn to use language in this way, our whole awareness and understanding shifts. We start to see each other, and the world, in new ways. What was invisible becomes visible. What was impossible becomes possible. And what was unknown to others—our unique "voice" and individual capacity to contribute to the greater good—becomes active, accessible, known.

C. Otto Scharmer, a senior lecturer at MIT and an expert in organizational learning, offers a useful metaphor for this deeper level of understanding and awareness at the organizational level in his book *Theory U*. Scharmer, who grew up on a farm in Germany, remembers his father teaching him to see the fields they tilled with a wider lens. "Each field, he explained to me, has two aspects: the visible, what we see above the surface, and the invisible, or what is below the surface. The quality of the yield—the visible result—is a function of the quality of the soil, of those elements of the field that are mostly invisible to the eye."[7]

Scharmer believes we should see "social fields"[8] the same way. "Social fields are the *grounding condition*, the living soil from which grows that which only later becomes visible to the eye. And just as every good farmer focuses attention on sustaining and enhancing the quality of the soil, every good organizational leader focuses attention on sustaining and enhancing the quality of the social field—the 'farm' in which every responsible leader works day in and day out."[9]

Understood this way, the most "visible" aspects of a school culture are the things parents, educators, and students do, say, and see. Trophy cases. School bathrooms. Test scores. Cafeteria food. Uniforms. Policies. All are important indicators of a school's quality and commitment to young people. And because these cultural indicators are visible, they end up receiving the bulk of our attention.

By contrast, the "invisible" parts of a school culture are far more elusive—and essential—to the cultivation of a healthy learning environment. Scharmer describes these features as the inner conditions from which parents, educators, and students operate with each other. Our hopes and fears. Our emotions. The quality of our relationships with each other. The issues we have informally agreed never to discuss.

These factors are the deepest determinants of a school's success (or failure) at creating a high-functioning school. And yet precisely because they are invisible (and so much harder to work on), they tend not to factor into most school improvement plans.

The central challenge in any organizational culture, therefore, is to help people become more adept at different ways of seeing—and of being seen. "We need to learn to attend to both dimensions simultaneously," says Scharmer. "*What* we say, see, and do (our visible realm), and the *inner place* from which we operate (the invisible realm, in which our sources of attention reside and from which they operate)."[10]

Attending to both dimensions—and balancing individual and group needs—is an essential goal for any organization. When a school finds the right balance in its organizational culture, it encourages all people to discover the power and uniqueness of their own voices. It helps young people chart a navigable path on their ongoing journeys of personal development. It helps members of the school community foster more meaningful, trusting relationships with each other. And it turns the old maxim about young people on its head, by creating a learning environment based on the belief that all children deserve to be seen *and* heard.

Democracies, organizations, and healthy schools cannot function optimally without a high degree of participation and social trust. This is not, therefore, "add-on" work; it is the superordinate goal of any organization that wishes to bring out the best in its people.

INVISIBLE CHILDREN

As we all know, too many children attend school each day without a sense of their own unique voice—and perhaps even with a horrible certainty of their own invisibility.

Each April 20, we mark another anniversary of the Columbine massacre— our country's most iconic example of what happens when unstable students who feel silenced and marginalized undertake the most destructive of means to be seen and heard. The murders at Virginia Tech provide the most recent example of this desperation. Such acts of extreme violence are, thankfully, rare. They also remind us how explosively hopeless and isolating the feelings of invisibility and voicelessness can be. As Martin Luther King Jr. once observed, violence is the language of the unheard.

I was reminded of this a few years ago, on March 30, 2006, when I was reading about the French student riots over a proposed new employment law—later withdrawn by the government in the face of overwhelming pressure—that were nearing their peak. As of that day, two-thirds of France's universities were overrun by student demonstrators, on strike, or closed.

One of the protest's young leaders, a seventeen-year-old girl named Floreal Mangin, described waking up the first few days of the protest to burned cars in her neighborhood. Often, she said, as she watched her classmates do it, she would think about what it takes to make someone reach that point. "They were destroying their own neighborhoods," she said in *The Guardian*, "smashing their own families' cars, but they had no other way of telling the world they existed."

Her words remind me of the connection between the visible things we *do* (in this case, burning cars), and the invisible emotions and ideas that spur us to *do* them (the need to announce our existence in a world that seems not to see us).

Again I thought of Columbine. Like these French youths, Eric Harris and Dylan Klebold lived in a world where words and language were useless, unreliable tools for them. Their choices were different, but the motivation behind their destructive acts, it seems to me, was similar—they felt they had no other way of telling the world they existed.

That's a type of hopelessness that can only result in desperation, anger, and resignation. I read later in the article that the rallying cry for these young French protesters was not the familiar, optimistic refrain uttered at American rallies for decades ("What do we want? When do we want it?")—it was, "WE ARE DISPOSABLE PIECES OF SHIT."

Recently, my musings about visibility led me back to my bookshelf and the novel that first introduced me to the concept, Ralph Ellison's classic, *Invisible Man*. (The first time I encountered the book, I was a high school freshman and I took the title literally—all I could think of was the old horror film in which a mad doctor wraps himself in bandages in order to be seen.)

Ellison's book begins by telling the story of an African American boy growing up in the Jim Crow South. Before he can fully understand himself and the larger world, the boy must first discover he is invisible to the white town leaders he is so eager to impress.

In an essay at the front of my edition, Ellison said this: "If the ideal of achieving a true political equality eludes us in reality—as it continues to do—there is still available that fictional *vision* of a democracy in which the actual combines with the ideal and gives us representations of a state of things in which the highly placed and the lowly, the black and the white, the Northerner and the Southerner, the native-born and the immigrant are combined to tell us of transcendent truths and possibilities such as those discovered when Mark Twain set Huck and Jim afloat on the raft."[11]

"A democracy in which the actual combines with the ideal": for Ellison, that was where fiction came in. For parents and educators, that's where our public schools, and our faith in the idea that all children deserve to be seen and heard, must come together.

How do schools create such environments? How do we cultivate the organizational "topsoil" where the visible and invisible social fields meet, connect, and intertwine? And how do we foster cultures that honor individual freedom *and* civic responsibility and ensure that all members of the community have the understanding, motivation, and skills they need to become active, visible contributors to the common good?

To do so, I believe we need an actionable framework for school leadership—one that helps us acknowledge the inner needs of everyone, is predicated on student learning and the meaningful inclusion of all voices, and helps us strike the right balance between individual freedom and group structure.

In the pages that follow, I will ground that challenging task in five skills I believe school leaders must cultivate, in themselves and in others, to create the conditions (the "fertile topsoil") that can best support a healthy, democratic, high-functioning school community.

Reflect. Connect. Create. Equip. Let Come.

NOTES

1. Linda Darling-Hammond, *The Right to Learn* (San Francisco: Jossey-Bass, 1997), 47, 16.
2. Stephen R. Covey, *The Eighth Habit* (New York: Free Press, 2005), 17.
3. James E. Zull, *The Art of Changing the Brain* (Sterling, VA: Stylus Publishing, 2002), 63.
4. Myles Horton, *The Long Haul* (New York & London: Teacher's College Press, 1998), 68, 227.
5. Allen Grossman, quoted in "Writing and Well-Being," *TriQuarterly* 75 (Spring–Summer 1989): p. 5.
6. Francisco Varela, quoted in Joseph Jaworksi, *Synchronicity: The Inner Path of Leadership* (San Francisco: Berrett-Koehler, 1998), 177.
7. C. Otto Scharmer, *Theory U: Leading From the Future as it Emerges* (Cambridge, MA: SOL, 2007), 8.
8. Scharmer defines a social field as "the totality of connections through which the participants of a given system relate, converse, think and act together." *Theory U*, 8.
9. Scharmer, *Theory U*, 8–9.
10. Scharmer, *Theory U*, 10.
11. Ralph Ellison, *Invisible Man* (New York: Vintage International, 1990), xx.

Part I

THEORY

Chapter One

Reflect
(or, take the time to know "who's there")

For three days in the Amherst College Gallery, faculty, students, and staff drew portraits from nine projected ink drawings. The resulting artifacts, each twelve feet high and ten feet wide, were examples of reflection and action, dialogue and meditation.

No great improvements in the lot of mankind are possible until a great change takes place in the fundamental constitution of their modes of thought.

—John Stuart Mill

When I was a teacher in Brooklyn, I loved reading *Hamlet* with my high school seniors.

The title character and my students were kindred spirits. Hamlet is, like most teenagers, a searcher, occasionally brooding and introspective. He has visions of his future that don't align with the visions the adults in his life have for him. He is an artist, an actor, and a dreamer—a person more comfortable in the world of words than the world of actions. And he is in love.

But Hamlet is also the future king of Denmark, which means he is bound by custom to avenge his father's murder—a duty that leads to his untimely death, in no small part because the act of killing goes against his very being.

No matter your age, then, to read the play is to watch a fellow human being struggle between staying true to his nature or accepting the role society has assigned him. This is part of the reason *Hamlet* has attracted more commentary than any other work in English except the Bible. But Hamlet's struggle also illuminates an essential question of human nature, not coincidentally posed by the first two words of the play—"Who's there?"

This is not a question many of us choose to ask of ourselves. Instead, we keep busy with work and other distractions. We ignore the inherent, unarticulated contradictions between our internal passions and our external actions. And we wonder why we are left feeling unfulfilled.

Everything we do is determined by who we think we are. And yet part of Hamlet's challenge is that throughout his struggle, his only recourse for greater self-understanding is to "unpack [his] heart with words."

This tension between thoughts, words, and actions continues throughout the play. At one point, Hamlet finds himself standing directly behind the man who killed his father—the king's brother Claudius. All the young prince needs to do is unsheathe his sword and complete his duty. But Hamlet feels paralyzed, even as he struggles to talk himself into it. He tries to "suit the action to the word, the word to the action"—but to no effect. Later, Hamlet bemoans the futility of "words, words, words"—at once his greatest resource and his chief source of frustration.

Shakespeare's exploration of the relationship between thoughts, words, and actions illuminates a universal human tension and a particular challenge of leadership: Before any of us can use our talents to make ourselves seen and heard, we must first understand how to "suit the action to the word, [and] the word to the action." And before we can ever hope to become the most effective teacher, parent, boss, or school leader, we must be willing to do the internal, reflective work necessary to answer the question, "Who's there?"

"TO THINE OWN SELF BE TRUE."

The line above is one of the most famous in *Hamlet*. I believe Shakespeare intended it to be read ironically—not because he didn't support the sentiment, but because human beings rarely achieve such a state of self-awareness.

The words belong to Polonius, a councilor to the new king and the father of Ophelia and Laertes. They are uttered while Polonius lectures his son before Laertes leaves Denmark for adventures abroad. Although I have seen the scene staged a number of different ways, as you listen to the father deliver a comically long list of things his son should keep in mind—"Give thy thoughts no tongue," "Be thou familiar, but by no means vulgar," "Give every man thy ear, but few thy voice," and so on, punctuated by the final piece of advice, "This above all; to thine own self be true"—it seems Shakespeare is underscoring a key theme of the play: Young people are too often told how to act and what to think. Moments later, as if to erase any doubts of interpretation, Shakespeare has Ophelia confess to her father, "I do not know, my lord, what I should think." "Marry, I will teach you," the father replies. "Think yourself a baby."

Polonius's overbearing relationship with his children provides a fitting intergenerational archetype for a play about the struggle for freedom and self-understanding. His advice, however—properly understood and applied—still carries great meaning. It also underscores a threshold pair of questions any leader intent on becoming more reflective must answer: To what must I stay true? What is my personal vision?

Most of us live our lives absent a fully defined personal vision. We may have goals and objectives. A vision, however, transcends objectives. It is larger than we are. When we find and pursue it, we may even feel we are being carried along by a force greater than ourselves.

Dr. Mihály Csíkszentmihályi, a psychology professor at Claremont Graduate University, describes this experience as "flow" and explains that the path toward achieving it begins with acquiring control over the contents of our own consciousness. "Getting control of life is never easy," he writes, "and sometimes it can be definitely painful. But in the long run optimal experiences add up to a sense of mastery—or perhaps better, a sense of *participation* in determining the content of life—that comes as close to what is usually meant by happiness as anything else we can conceivably imagine."[1]

Peter Senge, MIT's director of the Center for Organizational Learning, sees vision as separate from the concept of "purpose" as well. "Purpose is similar to a direction, a general heading," he says. "Vision is a specific destination, a picture of a desired future. Purpose is abstract. Vision is concrete. Purpose is 'advancing man's capability to explore the heavens.' Vision is 'a man on the moon by the end of the 1960s.'"[2] Both are necessary ingredients, Senge says . But "it can truly be said that nothing happens until there is vision."[3]

Whether we teach, run a business, or make art, the work we do—if it is to be truly fulfilling—must connect in some way to a larger vision we find meaningful. This deep sense of meaning is not alien to educators; most of us became teachers because we felt called to the profession, the children, and the work. Why, then, do so many leave the profession or remain in it but feel unfulfilled? Is it because we have become separated from that missionary spirit over time? Imagine the collective power of a school where all educators proactively worked to reconnect to that spirit—and all in the interest of improving the learning conditions for young people?

In the prologue, I shared the vision driving my own work: that one day, no child will feel invisible at school, and all children will have the skills and self-confidence they need to be seen and heard in meaningful, responsible ways. Perhaps some variation of this vision is also meaningful to you. What matters most is discovering the core idea that will drive and sustain us. Once we do, our professional work shifts from a tendency toward narrow, unemotional goals (e.g., raising student test scores to meet annual yearly progress) to a broader, all-encompassing personal vision (unleashing human potential and making all children feel visible).

This does not mean schools simply need to organize a schoolwide shared visioning process that results in a new mission statement. Nothing undermines the creative and participative processes more than the naïve belief that all a good vision needs is implementation and rollout. It does mean we should always begin with a clear commitment to understand what drives us as professionals and as human beings.

As organizational theorist Meg Wheatley has said, great leaders begin with a strong intention, not a set of action plans. Therefore, if I want to encourage a more democratic organizational culture at my school, there's nothing I as a leader need to brand or categorize or get people to "buy into" right away. The first step is simply to be more intentional about how I reflect on who I am and why I do what I do. My long-range goal, from an organizational perspective, is to cultivate a climate in which it's safe for all people to articulate what is meaningful, ask questions, offer ideas, and respectfully challenge the status quo. And my daily goal is to model the behavior I want to see in others.

"WORDS, WORDS, WORDS"

It's one thing to recognize that self-reflection and internal clarity is an essential quality of leadership. It's another to begin thinking about how to cultivate that sort of clarity, both personally and across an organization of individuals.

In this regard we are all, to some degree, like Hamlet: our most useful tools and chief sources of frustration are the "words, words, words" we use, and our capacity to choose the right ones to generate a clearer alignment between what we value and how we live our lives. Yet finding the right words and reflecting on the quality of one's work do not play major roles in the organizational culture of most schools or in the leadership development of most principals.

It has, however, been a subject of intense focus in the private sector for some time. As Harvard Business School professor Chris Argyris writes, "Most people define learning too narrowly as mere 'problem solving.' But if learning is to persist, managers and employees must also look inward. They need to reflect critically on their own behavior, identify the ways they often inadvertently contribute to the organization's problems, and then change how they act."[4]

Developing the reflective skills and the language to break out of this sort of cycle takes time, but it is possible—at both the individual and organizational levels. "Despite the strength of defensive reasoning, people genuinely strive to produce what they intend," Argyris explains. "They value acting competently. Their self-esteem is intimately tied up with behaving consistently and performing effectively."

Each of us can rely on these universal human tendencies to learn how to think in a new way. "People can be taught how to recognize the reasoning they use when they design and implement their actions," says Argyris. "They can begin to identify the inconsistencies between their espoused and actual theories of action. They can face up to the fact that they unconsciously design and implement actions that they do not intend. Finally, people can learn how to identify what individuals and groups do to create organizational defenses and how these defenses contribute to an organization's problems."[5]

A personal story comes to mind. When I was teaching in Brooklyn, I was also hired to coach the school's basketball team. In retrospect, I now see I fell into a pattern of mimicking my own high school coach—a man who yelled and berated his players mercilessly. I hated this leadership style, and yet I unconsciously reenacted it when I became a coach. It was as if I had no other behavioral model to call on, so I repeated the only one I knew, despite my desire to do otherwise.

Argyris describes this as the difference between our espoused theory of action ("I am a fun, compassionate coach") and our actual theory-in-use ("I berate as often as I praise"). "Put simply," he says, "people consistently act inconsistently, unaware of the contradiction between their espoused theory and their theory-in-use, between the way they think they are acting and the way they really act."[6]

School principals reading this may have already identified a few members of their staff for whom this description fits perfectly. But it is always essential that we start with ourselves. As leaders, our threshold challenge is not to identify the shortcomings of the most troublesome teachers or students but to be certain we can recognize our own shortcomings—and guard against projecting them onto others via the words we choose and the decisions we make.

Argyris believes we all design our actions according to four basic values: to remain in unilateral control; to maximize winning and minimize losing; to suppress negative feelings; and to be as rational as possible—by which people mean defining clear objectives and evaluating their behavior in terms of whether or not they have achieved them. Because the purpose of each value is to avoid embarrassment or vulnerability, many of our interactions end up being highly defensive.

Once this sort of thinking is exposed and examined, however, people start to "see" their own thinking as it develops. As organizational consultant Adam Kahane has observed, "We are accustomed to believing that there is a world 'out there' that exists apart from us and that we can see and manipulate objectively. But modern cognitive science teaches us that cognition is not a representation of an independent, pregiven world, but rather a bringing forth of the world. What is brought forth by a particular organism in the process of living is not *the* world but *a* world, one that is always dependent on the organism."[7]

Words, in other words—and the way we use them to frame meetings, conversations, and our private interpretations of the world around us—matter greatly. "We can never help address a problem situation from a comfortable position of uninvolved innocence," Kahane explains. "If we want to help, we must first understand and acknowledge our role—by commission or omission—in creating the situation."[8]

UNDERSTANDING HOW WE LEARN

One way to make our thought process visible is by assessing our individual learning and leadership style. As numerous studies have shown, there is a natural cycle to learning, mirrored in the geography of the brain. This cycle begins with our perceptions, which we then reflect upon and often compare to others' experiences. A conceptual understanding of the experience begins to be formed, after which we gather information, often from experts, before trying out our new understanding.

By playing around with our developing understanding, we start to become ready to apply our new knowledge and skills to some personally meaningful endeavor. These actions, once taken, provide useful feedback as well as the opportunity to refine our understanding about how to integrate this new knowledge into our experiences.

According to Robert Kegan, a professor in adult learning at Harvard, each of us must go through the full cycle to experience true learning. Only then will new knowledge and skills be retained and ready for use to apply to novel situations and future learning opportunities.

If that sounds too abstract, think about it this way: our learning styles have a significant impact on how we each travel the learning cycle. These different styles, a combination of innate tendencies and learned behaviors, outline the interplay of our preferences for perceiving and processing information.

Bernice McCarthy's 4MAT system, a synthesis of numerous researchers' work, provides the most elegant and readily applied for our purposes. McCarthy identifies four archetypal learning styles: imaginative, analytic, common sense, and dynamic. The characteristics of each are derived largely from the intersection of two continua.

The first is how we perceive information and where we fall along the continuum of experiencing-feeling-thinking. Kim Carter, the founding director of Monadnock Community Connections School in Swanzey, New Hampshire (see chapter 8)—a school structured around 4MAT concepts—explained it to me this way:

> When my husband and I were buying our first house, I would walk through the empty rooms, picturing family dinners and bedtime stories. He would go immediately to the basement to check out the fuse box and furnace. We were each gathering our "essential" information about the prospective house, albeit from two different perspectives.

The second continuum is how we process the information we have taken in and the pace at which we move from reflective to active processing. Again, Kim Carter:

> As an eleven-month old in a new day care setting, my youngest son sat and watched the other children take the half step between the kitchen and the playroom for several minutes before trying to navigate the step himself. By contrast, my middle son had his older brother remove the training wheels from his bicycle so he could throw himself down a hill behind our house, over and over again, until he could stay up. Whereas one of my sons needed lots of internal processing before action, the other was more content to act immediately and process later.

In their most abstract forms, the 4MAT learning styles help chart the way we combine our preferences for perceiving and processing information.

Imaginative learners, for example, tend to perceive information through experiencing and feeling and then process reflectively. Analytic learners also process reflectively, but they perceive information conceptually by thinking the ideas through. Common sense learners also perceive information by thinking a lot, but they process actively. And dynamic learners process actively and perceive through experience.

Our style preferences have a lot to do with how we travel the learning cycle itself. The style we are strongest in is also the part of the learning cycle in which we feel most comfortable.

The best way to make sense of these ideas is to take a self-assessment. (You can do so at www.aboutlearning.com.) After completing the assessment you'll be given a number and an explanation of what that number means (see figure 1.1). Ones, for example, need to explore why something is important to learn and connect it to their own values. Twos enjoy receiving information, while threes want to use what they've learned. Fours, meanwhile, look to connect the information to other things they know.

It's important to underscore that no one is a pure "number"—to differing degrees, we have traces of all four styles. Furthermore, different situations can call for different style characteristics. As David Kolb states, learning style is a stable state, not a fixed trait.[9]

Our different learning styles shape our behavior as leaders as well. We each have natural preferences for our approach to interpersonal communication, although different situations will demand that we draw on different aspects of ourselves that may or may not reflect our strengths as learners and communicators. A big-picture person with an eye on using data to improve student achievement, for example, will also need to attend to the specific strategies required for making the desired improvements, as well as nurturing relationships and cultivating a shared commitment to the goal.

When our colleagues share a commitment to understanding personal styles and preferences, we can more readily depend on different people to attend to different needs and stay focused on our personal strengths. When we lack this awareness, we are more likely to feel the need to stretch ourselves in ways that will not serve the greater good.

DEVELOPING A CULTURE OF CRITICAL FRIENDSHIP

Helping each other reflect on the quality of our work is a crucial task that often gets squeezed out by other, seemingly more pressing duties. This is a particular challenge for school leaders, who must somehow allocate the time, amid all the other competing pressures, to cultivate a culture of reflection. As

Type Four Leader

- Is **dynamic** and **enthusiastic**.
- Seeks alignment between **what is and what might be**.
- Relies primarily on **intuition** for decision making.
- **Judges** others by their **enthusiasm**, their liveliness.
- Expects people to act on their world in **ever-widening circles**.
- Often **communicates poorly** because of expectations that **people should know what to do** and a preoccupation with the present that leads to **forgetfulness of past communications**.
- Works well with **staff who are quick**, both in thought and action, **and who can follow up** and implement details.
- Tackles problems by **intuiting possibilities** and **taking risks**.
- Has **difficulty tolerating people who don't see what needs** to be done.
- Is **flexible and open, yet** firmly set in **deeply held values**, which causes inner conflict.
- Works to enhance **organization's reputation as a front runner**.
- Creates **opportunities**.
- Exercises authority by holding up a **vision of what might be**.
- Leads by **energizing** people.
- Thrives on **change**.
- Focuses on **vision** as primary structure.
- **Needs** others to provide details and **follow-through**.
- Communication strength is articulating **the big picture**.

Type One Leader

- Is **empowering** and **involved**.
- Seeks alignment between **personal and organizational values**.
- Relies primarily on **consensus** and **support** in decision making.
- **Judges** others by **how they treat people**.
- Expects people to **grow in self-awareness**.
- Is a **good communicator** but sometimes **focuses on feelings** at the expense of the message.
- Works well with **supportive staff** who share the sense of mission
- Tackles problems by first **verifying perceptions** and **possible solutions** with others.
- Has **difficulty tolerating inconsiderate** people.
- Experiences **inner conflict** when the organization's behavior/structure is in conflict with its values.
- Works to enhance **organizational solidarity**.
- Creates a sense of **community**.
- Exercises authority with **trust** and **participation**.
- Leads by **articulating** and **acting on** the mission.
- **Thrives on developing** good ideas.
- Relies on **group values** as primary structure.
- **Needs** others to provide **consensus**.
- Communication strategy is **active listening**.

Type Three Leader

- Is **productive** and **action-oriented**.
- Seeks alignment between **goals and output**.
- Relies primarily on **results** for decision making.
- **Judges** others by their **straightforwardness** and **hard work**.
- Expects people to seek **increasing competence**.
- Often has **communication difficulties** because of a straightforward manner that **tends to overlook people's feelings**.
- Works well with **staff who are task oriented** and **move quickly**.
- Tackles problems with **immediacy**, often without consulting others.
- Has **difficulty tolerating indecisiveness**.
- Is **strongly task oriented** which causes inner conflict because of deep people concerns.
- Works to enhance organization's **productivity** and **solvency**.
- Creates a **productive climate**, often pitching in and working side-by-side with co-workers.
- Exercises authority by demanding **bottom-line results**.
- Leads by **personal forcefulness**, inspiring **quality**.
- **Thrives on solving** difficult problems.
- Relies on **efficiency of output** as primary structure.
- **Needs** others to provide **teaming skills**.
- Communication strength is **directness**.

Type Two Leader

- Is **problem-focused** and **lively-minded**.
- Seeks alignment between **people and procedures**.
- Relies primarily on **data** for decision-making.
- **Judges** others by their **accomplishments**.
- Expects people to seek **increasing professional knowledge**.
- Is reluctant to speak **until all the facts are known**, which often causes **communication problems**.
- Works well with **staff who follow through**, are **well-organized**, and have things down **on paper**.
- Tackles problems with **logic** and **rationality**.
- Has **difficulty tolerating action without rational** basis.
- **Strives for perfection**, which coupled with **fear of failure**, causes inner conflict.
- Works to enhance organization's **reputation for prestige**.
- Creates a **solid organizational structure**.
- Exercises authority with **assertive persuasion**.
- Leads by **honoring** and implementing principles and **procedures**.
- **Thrives on understanding** and working **through** complex problems.
- Relies on **organized planning** as primary structure.
- **Needs** others to provide **impetus**.
- Communication strength is **precision in words** and **data**.

About Learning, Inc. 1251 N. Old Rand Rd, Wauconda, IL 60084 Phone 847.487.1800 • 1.800.822.4MAT • Fax 847.487.1811
From *The Leadership Behavior Inventory* by Bernice McCarthy and Suzanne Sanders. ©2000 About Learning, Inc. All rights reserved. No reproduction allowed.

Figure 1.1.   About Learning's four archetypal learning styles.

Meg Wheatley writes, "The leader's role is not to make sure that people know exactly what to do and when to do it. Instead, leaders need to ensure that there is strong evolving clarity about who the organization is."[10]

Daniel Baron, a thirty-year veteran of education and school reform and the founder of the Project School in Bloomington, Indiana, has seen the positive results of this sort of organizational clarity. He believes the key to changing teachers' behaviors is getting them in touch with their own beliefs and the shared beliefs of their colleagues—and then letting them self-diagnose the gaps in their professional practice. "It is the principal's responsibility," he asserts, "to uncover, recover, or discover the community's core beliefs so the educational experience for students is cohesive, is intentional, and maintains a high level of professional integrity. Once a school community is clear about its vision, mission, and moral purpose, it is not only possible but also highly likely that the community will found itself on a culture of critical friendship."[11]

The Critical Friends Group (CFG) process, first developed by the Annenberg Institute for School Reform at Brown University,[12] focuses on developing collegial relationships, encouraging reflective practice, and rethinking the role of school leadership. The process is designed to build a culture of equity and cooperative adult learning—an approach that runs contrary to most adult work environments.

"Critical friends take an interest in one another's core beliefs and the commonly held beliefs of the learning community," Baron explains. They support one another in closing the gap between their beliefs and practices and hold one another accountable for continually adapting their practice to meet the needs of all learners, sharing resources and ideas, and supporting one another as they take risks to improve their practices. They commit themselves to:

- Be reflective
- Make their teaching practices public to one another
- Frame meaningful questions and ask for substantive feedback from one another
- Hold one another accountable for meeting the needs of students who struggle the most
- Ask the kinds of questions that provoke and challenge their assumptions and habits
- Believe that together they are more capable of knowing what they need to know and learning what they need to learn than they are alone.

"To nurture a culture of critical friendship," Baron says, "the principal must model relationships with his or her faculty members that are founded on mutual trust and freedom from judgment. The principal must also support the teachers' ability to freely discuss one another's work with the intention of improving the learning for each student. Critical friendship starts from the inside of one's identity as an educator and develops into professional relationships that can last a lifetime."[13]

To help schools create these sorts of cultures, the National School Reform Faculty (NSRF) provides training in the use of a long list of protocols and processes that consist of agreed-upon guidelines for specific purposes. They can be used for learning from looking at student and educator work, giving feedback, observing one another's teaching or leadership practice, or discussing professional articles. By using them as a way to frame important work, educators can, as Baron puts it, "build collegial skills and habits; ensure equity in participation; reflect and listen for understanding; and support the development of a sustainable, collaborative school culture."[14]

These CFG principles were on display one recent August morning in the tiny town of Mathis, Texas, where school superintendent Luis Gonzalez had invited NSRF to provide three days of professional development[15] around the use of CFG protocols. As the 300-some adults (about 6 percent of the town's population) sat in the rectangular multipurpose room eating a hot breakfast, Gonzalez welcomed them back from their summer breaks and tried to capture the goals of the work ahead. "What we're trying to do," he said, "is create a community together."

Following breakfast, the teachers broke into smaller groups of fifteen. Daniel, facilitating one of the groups, opened the meeting with an exercise, Origins of My Name, in which each person takes a few minutes to think about the origin of his or her name(s) and sees what stories emerge. In pairs, people briefly share their stories. Then the whole group gathers to learn about each other, with each person's story retold by the partner who just heard it.

During the exercise, colleagues who had worked together for decades learned new insights about each other, and the mood of the group became more noticeably relaxed and open. Before moving on, Daniel asked the group a question he repeatedly posed over the next three days: "How could you use an activity like this in your classroom?" Victor, a clean-cut, silver-haired former military man who has been teaching in Mathis since 1992, replied first. "This is a great way to get to know each other, and a different way to think about ourselves."

Later that day, Daniel introduced the group to another CFG process, the Collaborate Assessment Conference (CAC). "The CAC protocol (see figure 1.2)," he explained, "is designed to provide a structure by which teachers come together to look at a piece of student work, first to determine what it reveals about the student and the issues s/he cares about, and then to consider how the student's issues and concerns relate to the teacher's goals for the child."

The structure for the CAC evolved from three key ideas: First, students use school assignments, especially open-ended ones, to tackle important

National
School
Reform
Faculty

Harmony
Education   www.nsrfharmony.org
Center

Collaborative Assessment Conference Protocol

Developed by Steve Seidel and colleagues at Harvard Project Zero

1. Getting Started
- The group chooses a facilitator who will make sure the group stays focused on the particular issue addressed in each step.
- The presenting teacher puts the selected work in a place where everyone can see it or provides copies for the other participants. S/he says nothing about the work, the context in which it was created, or the student, until Step 5.
- The participants observe or read the work in silence, perhaps making brief notes about aspects of it that they particularly notice.

2. Describing the Work
- The facilitator asks the group, "What do you see?"
- Group members provide answers without making judgments about the quality of the work or their personal preferences.
- If a judgment emerges, the facilitator asks for the evidence on which the judgment is based.

3. Asking Questions About the Work
- The facilitator asks the group, "What questions does this work raise for you?"
- Group members state any questions they have about the work, the child, the assignment, the circumstances under which the work was carried out, and so on.
- The presenting teacher may choose to make notes about these questions, but s/he is does not respond to them now--nor is s/he obligated to respond to them in Step 5 during the time when the presenting teacher speaks.

4. Speculating About What the Student Is Working On
- The facilitator asks the group, "What do you think the child is working on?"
- Participants, based on their reading or observation of the work, make suggestions about the problems or issues that the student might have been focused on in carrying out the assignment.

5. Hearing from the Presenting Teacher
- The facilitator invites the presenting teacher to speak.
- The presenting teacher provides his or her perspective on the student's work, describing what s/he sees in it, responding (if s/he chooses) to one or more of the questions raised, and adding any other information that s/he feels is important to share with the group.
- The presenting teacher also comments on anything surprising or unexpected that s/he heard during the describing, questioning and speculating phases.

6. Discussing Implications for Teaching and Learning
- The facilitator invites everyone (the participants and the presenting teacher) to share any thoughts they have about their own teaching, children's learning, or ways to support this particular child in future instruction.

7. Reflecting on the Collaborative Assessment Conference
- The group reflects on the experiences of or reactions to the conference as a whole or to particular parts of it.

8. Thanks to the Presenting Teacher

Protocols are most powerful and effective when used within an ongoing professional learning community such as a Critical Friends Group® and facilitated by a skilled coach. To learn more about professional learning communities and seminars for new or experienced coaches, please visit the National School Reform Faculty website at www.nsrfharmony.org.

Figure 1.2

problems in which they are personally interested. Sometimes these problems are the same ones that the teacher has assigned them to work on, sometimes not. Second, we can only begin to see and understand the serious work that students undertake if we suspend judgment long enough to look carefully and closely at what is actually in the work rather than what we hope to see in it. Third, we need the perspective of others—especially those who are not intimate with our goals for our students—to help us see aspects of the student and the work that would otherwise escape us, and we need others to help us generate ideas about how to use this information to shape our daily practice.

In the CACs that day, a number of very different examples of student work were shared: One woman brought a geometry definition quiz on which most students scored poorly. Nearby, a cheery elementary school teacher named Jennifer shared a short writing sample of a struggling student who had already been left back a grade.

Jennifer was restricted from saying anything at all throughout the first half of the conference—she could give no information about the student, the assignment, or the context in which the student completed it. This was clearly difficult for Jennifer, who seemed eager to share her insights about this student, and of what she was trying to elicit from this particular assignment.

What followed was a series of questions in which Daniel led the rest of the group through an exploration of the work. First, the group described Jennifer's student's writing sample in detail ("I see a real variety of word choice here," "This student consistently uses correct punctuation," etc.), and the group searched for clues that might suggest gaps or problems ("I wonder if this student had seen examples of what would constitute 'A' work," "I wonder if this is typical or atypical work for this student," etc.), as well as areas in which the student seems particularly engaged. The group did all of this without judgment, thanks largely to the work of Daniel, who continually reminded each participant to identify the evidence on which his or her statements were based. At one point, when Victor observed that the student seemed confused about what to do, Daniel asked him to point to specific evidence in the work that supported that assumption. Only observations that could be grounded in evidence were allowed to move forward for greater consideration by the group.

In the second half of the conference, the focus broadened. Jennifer was welcomed back into the conversation as an active participant, and the group built on its examination of the piece by hearing how the work was created, along with other relevant information about the student and the assignment.

It was an emotional coaching session for Jennifer. Through tears, she thanked the group for helping her see her own assessment process from a broader lens. "This young man," she explained, "is such a well-meaning student, but he struggles so much that I've been wondering how I could provide positive feedback. You have helped me see how hard he worked to complete the assignment—and where I can give him honest, constructive feedback without feeling so deflated by his ongoing challenges."

The conference concluded with Daniel asking the group to reflect together on the ideas they had heard. "I understand now that this is really about creating a different way of seeing," said one veteran teacher. "It feels like we were able to achieve two goals: we helped a colleague see her assignment and the student's work from a broader perspective than she could ever hope to by herself, and we worked with a structured process that freed us to have a more honest conversation about the student work, but also the learning process in general."

Another NSRF process is designed to help colleagues analyze how a successful professional practice has developed so that the group can apply any lessons learned toward its future endeavors. The Success Analysis Protocol (see figure 1.3) begins with each participant taking a few minutes to reflect on and then write a short description of a successful project in which they've participated. In smaller groups of three, each person presents his or her personal project story while the rest of the group takes notes on what they hear. Afterward, the listeners ask clarifying questions about the details of the best practice and discuss—without the presenter's participation—what they feel made the experience successful. Then all three people talk about the key attributes of the success story and how these insights might be applied to future work.

In this way, the purpose of the protocol is not simply to generate happy talk, but to use personal observations as valuable data toward the proactive improvement of one's professional practice. And in both cases, the process of participating in CFG protocols is akin to co-creating narratives that help people better understand what is already working, what still needs to be done, and what should happen next.

Indeed, the Success Analysis Protocol and others like it encourage a different sort of data-driven decision making by giving professionals an opportunity to share their stories, hear the stories of others, and reflect together on the words, images, and metaphors heard. Recent insights in the field of cognitive science confirm why this is such an effective strategy. As James Zull explains in *The Art of Changing the Brain*, "Recalling and creating stories are key parts of learning. We remember by connecting things with our stories, we create by connecting our stories together in unique and memorable ways, and we act out our stories in our behaviors. If you believe . . . that learning is deepest when it engages the most parts of the brain," Zull writes, "you can see the value of stories for the teacher. We should tell stories, create stories, and repeat stories, and we should ask our students to do the same."[16]

National
School
Reform
Faculty

Harmony
Education   www.nsrfharmony.org
Center

The Success Analysis Protocol
Extended Version

Developed in the field by educators affiliated with NSRF.

Purpose of this protocol
To analyze how a new successful practice has developed so that we can apply the lessons learned to future work.

Roles
A timekeeper/facilitator to help the group stay focused on how the practice described by the presenter is different from more routine practices. The analysis of what makes this practice so successful is the purpose of the protocol. The facilitator is a full participant in this protocol.

"Best Practice" is defined as a process that proved to be highly effective in achieving the intended outcome.

1. Identifying a success. Reflect on and then write a short description of a "best practice" that you have developed over the last year. (5 minutes)

2. Presenter describes the success. In groups of 3, the first person shares his or her "best practice". The rest of group takes notes. (3 minutes)

3. Group asks clarifying questions. The rest of the group asks clarifying questions about the details of the "best practice". (3 minutes)

4. Group reflects on the success story. The group discusses what they heard the presenter describing. What helped the experience to be so successful? (5 minutes)
   Note: Presenter does not participate in this part of the discussion but does take notes.

5. Presenter responds. The presenter responds to the group's discussion of what made this learning experience so successful and how it might be applied to future work. (3 minutes)
   Note: Presenter does not have to respond to questions raised in Step 4.

6. Appreciate! Take a moment to appreciate the good work of your colleague. (1 minute)

7. Each member takes a turn sharing. Repeat steps 2 through 6 for each member of the group. Remember to keep the focus on *the process that helped to make the experience so successful.* (15 minutes each)

8. Debrief the protocol as a whole group. Possible questions; what worked well? How might we apply what we learned to other work? (5 minutes)

Protocols are most powerful and effective when used within an ongoing professional learning community such as a Critical Friends Group® and facilitated by a skilled coach. To learn more about professional learning communities and seminars for new or experienced coaches, please visit the National School Reform Faculty website at www.nsrfharmony.org.

Figure 1.3

In part, Hamlet's story ends so tragically because it was written not by him, but by the expectations of the society in which he lived. Educators today are not similarly constrained (despite how it may feel). But we still need to learn how to use words and language to tell the right stories—the ones that connect us to our personal experiences and passions. We need to learn to ask the right questions—the ones that help us create healthier, higher-functioning work environments. We have to trust what we discover. "And this above all; to thine own self be true."

REFLECT—FIVE THINGS YOU CAN DO

Read *Finding Our Way*

Finding Our Way is a collection of organizational theorist Margaret Wheatley's articles. Wheatley applies themes she has addressed throughout her career to detail organizational practices and behaviors that bring more reflective, functional learning environments to life.

"The pieces presented here," she writes, "represent more than ten years of work, of how I took the ideas in my books and applied them in practice in many different situations. However, this is more than a collection of articles. I updated, revised or substantially added to the original content of each one. In this way, everything written here represents my most current views on these subjects."

Keep a Blog on the Network at fivefreedoms.org

The network at fivefreedoms.org provides an online forum for people committed to First Amendment freedoms, democratic schools, and the idea that children should be seen and heard. Visit the network to set up your own personal profile, and then use the blog feature to regularly share your ideas and observations about your own professional practices—or take a few minutes to read the insights of others.

To set up a profile, visit http://network.fivefreedoms.org.

Become Skilled in Critical Friendship

The National School Reform Faculty (NSRF) is a professional development initiative that focuses on developing collegial relationships, encouraging reflective practice, and rethinking leadership in restructuring schools—all in support of increased student achievement.

At the heart of NSRF's program are the concepts of Facilitative Leadership and Critical Friendship. AS NSRF explains, "We have learned that Critical Friendship, an essential ingredient for learning communities, is best achieved through providing deliberate time and structures to promote adult growth that is directly linked to student learning. Facilitative Leadership skills are needed to engage school communities in this practice, and are valuable for all leaders—school leaders, classroom teachers and district administrators."

To learn more about NSRF, and to access its rich list of dialogue protocols, visit www.nsrfharmony.org.

(Slowly) Think a New Way into Being

You can help this process along by asking yourself a few reflective questions and then visually representing your answers in some way—a journal, a drawing, etc.

1. What in your life and work are the situations, practices, and activities that connect you most with your best sources of energy and inspiration?
2. Consider these activities and situations as small seeds and building blocks of the future: What might a possible future look like in which these small seeds and building blocks are interconnected and grow into an inspiring whole that resonates with your best energies?
3. If you were to bring that future into the world, what would you need to let go of? What, in other words, are the old habits that must die in order for something new to emerge?
4. If you took the risk and this project failed, what would be the worst-case scenario, and would you be ready to face it?

Conduct Stakeholder Interviews

Regularly reserve time to spend with key stakeholders and have a conversation with them in which you actively work to walk in their shoes and see your job (and behavior) from their point of view. Here are four questions you might use, derived from Otto Scharmer's book *Theory U*, to frame the discussion:

1. What is your most important goal here, and how can I help you achieve it?
2. What criteria will you use to determine whether my contributions to your work have been successful or not?
3. If I tried to change two things I'm responsible for with regard to your own work, which things would be of the greatest value and benefit for you?
4. Are there any historic barriers that have traditionally made it difficult for people with my job to support you and your work? If so, what is it that keeps getting in your way?

NOTES

1. Mihály Csíkszentmihályi, *Flow* (London & Sydney: Rider, 1992), 4.

2. Peter Senge, *The Fifth Discipline* (New York & London: Doubleday, 2006), 138.

3. Ibid.

4. Chris Argyris, "Teaching Smart People How to Learn," *Harvard Business Review* (May–June 1991): p. 6.

5. Ibid., 12.

6. Ibid., 12.

7. Adam Kahane, *Solving Tough Problems* (San Francisco: Berrett-Kohler, 2004, 2007), 84.

8. Ibid., 84.

9. David Kolb, *Experiential Learning: Experience as the Source of Learning and Development* (Upper Saddle River, NJ: Prentice-Hall, 1984), 63.

10. Margaret Wheatley, *Leadership and the New Science* (San Francisco: Berrett-Kohler, 2006), 131.

11. Daniel Baron, "Critical Friendship: Leading From the Inside Out," *Principal Leadership* (May 2007): 56–58. Quote on p. 56.

12. In July 2000, the National School Reform Faculty program, which currently houses Critical Friends Groups and coordinates the training for Critical Friends Coaches, relocated to the Harmony School Education Center (HSEC) in Bloomington, Indiana. On September 1, 2009, the faculty members of the National School Reform Faculty began a new independent organization, School Reform Initiative (SRI), to carry on the work of critical friendship within intentional learning communities. All the protocols and other strategies referenced in this text can also be found on the SRI website, www.schoolreforminitiative.org.

13. Baron, "Critical Friendship," 57.

14. Ibid.

15. In addition to the three initial days of work, NSRF agreed to provide two one-day follow-up meetings, alongside three or four other sessions throughout the year.

16. James E. Zull, *The Art of Changing the Brain* (Sterling, VA: Stylus Publishing, 2002), 228.

Chapter Two

Connect
(or, make the connections
that let you "see the whole board")

Participants from the Amherst community continued the process of nine collaborative drawings. Contrary to the traditional Western understanding that "art" is a noun, this activity was a collective vision in which "art" was understood as a verb.

> Our talking and listening often fails to solve complex problems because of
> the way that most of us talk and listen most of the time. Our most common
> way of talking is telling: asserting the truth about the way things are and
> must be, not allowing that there might be other truths and possibilities.
> And our most common way of listening is not listening: listening only to
> our own talking, not to others. This way of talking and listening works
> fine for solving simple problems. . . . But a complex problem can only be
> solved if the people who are part of the problem work together creatively
> to understand their situation and how to improve it.
>
> — Adam Kahane

I admit it—I'm a *West Wing* junkie.

My wife and I have watched every minute of every season—often in bunches, thanks to the binge-enabling wonder of Netflix. My favorite comes from the third season. It's called "Hartsfield's Landing," a fictional reference to the small town in New Hampshire (Dixfield Notch, just forty-two registered voters) that is the first in the country to cast ballots in the presidential primaries. The overarching theme of the episode, however, is less about the science of politics and more about the art of leadership—specifically, the skill of "seeing the whole board."

It begins with President Bartlet having just returned from a trip to India, where he and regional leaders were discussing the ongoing dispute over the region of Kashmir. "We also had a spirited conversation about chess," Bartlet tells the press corps huddled outside Air Force One. "Chess was invented in India. Somewhere around 600 A.D., a gigantic chessboard was constructed, and human figures were used as chess pieces."

For those of you that have never watched the show, it's worth noting President Bartlet is a reservoir of obscure facts. But his history lesson gets interrupted when Leo, the president's chief of staff, summons Bartlet back to the White House. Taiwan and China, Leo reports, are on the verge of a major conflict over Taiwan's decision to test fire a U.S.-made Patriot missile.

"We have a pretty good sense of the worst-case scenario?" Bartlet asks.

"We end up sending the largest naval armada to Southeast Asia since the end of Vietnam," Leo answers.

Thus begins the first of many "chess matches" in *West Wing* creator and head writer Aaron Sorkin's script. Bartlet, Leo, and the Joint Chiefs try to negotiate a peaceful resolution to the conflict between China and Taiwan. Two other characters stage a series of phone calls to a family in Hartsfield's Landing that may not vote for Bartlet (a significant defection in a town with so few residents). And the president plays two actual games of chess with two staffers to whom he has given extremely valuable sets as gifts.

Sorkin uses each match to reveal a different aspect of the president's personality and of the challenges of leadership. In one game, between the president and a brilliant young aide named Sam, Bartlet speaks candidly about the unfolding crisis in Taiwan. As he moves his wooden pieces on the board, Sam, thrilled his boss has let him "come inside" to witness the highest levels of diplomacy at work, tries to guess where the crisis is headed.

BARTLET: (*looking at the board*) Your move.

SAM: Hang on. . . . You've got two carrier groups headed to the Taiwan Strait. . . .

BARTLET: Move.

SAM: Plus, the USS *Carl Vincent* in the South China Sea . . . (*moves a figure on the board*). Beijing wants you to scale back the weapons and you're not going to do it. . . .

BARTLET: Right. (*takes one of Sam's chess pieces*)

SAM: How does it work?

BARTLET : See the whole board!

Bartlet is using the backdrop of the chess game to help equip a talented young aide with the skills he needs to see problems more systemically. Later, when Bartlet returns to resume the game, Sam shows the extent to which he has continued to consider the problem at hand.

BARTLET: Let's get back to it.

SAM: You know, sir, I looked something up while you were gone. Eisenhower, it seemed, at all costs wanted to avoid sending ships to resupply Quemoy and Matsu, because they'd be less than a mile from the Chinese army. A private could . . . well, everybody was a private in Mao's army, but a private could fire on a ship and that'd be it. We'd be at war. We'd have to be.

BARTLET: Yeah.

SAM: Eisenhower wouldn't do it.

BARTLET: No.

SAM: Why are you?

BARTLET: Look at the whole board.

SAM: I am.

BARTLET: You're not.

SAM: I'm trying!

BARTLET: *Sam. . . .*

SAM: Why were the carrier groups in the Taiwan Strait?

BARTLET: Are they in the Taiwan Strait?

SAM: They're on their way.

BARTLET: Is that the same thing?

SAM: How does this end?

Without giving away the answer, Taiwan and China do not go to war, and Sam is amazed at the way the conflict is skillfully averted. "I don't know how you do it," he says, to which the president responds:

> You have a lot of help. You listen to everybody and then you call the play. [He rises to his feet.] Sam. You're going to run for president one day. Don't be scared. You can do it. I believe in you.

Bartlet is not quick to praise his hard-working staff. He has chosen the perfect time to do so with Sam—shortly after he has written for his boss a memorable State of the Union address. It is the type of encounter that will strengthen the relationship between the two, increase Sam's self-confidence, and solidify the president's status as a worthy mentor.

At the same time, and in a different room, Bartlett plays chess with his communications director, Toby. Here, however, the balance of power is reversed, thanks to a recent comment of Toby's that has gotten under the president's skin.

The issue at hand is the president's public persona and whether he modifies his behavior to appeal to voters. A few days earlier, Toby challenged the president to be true to himself. As they play the game, Bartlet is still agitated as he furiously scoops up Toby's chess pieces.

BARTLET: (*responds with a move*) You think the strike against me is nobody likes the smartest kid in the class.

TOBY: I don't know, sir. Being the smartest kid in the class is a pretty good pitch. It's not a strike unless you watch it as it sails by.

BARTLET: I don't do that.

TOBY: Check.

BARTLET: And I'm not a snob.

TOBY: I don't believe you are.

Through the two chess matches, Aaron Sorkin shows us the dialectical nature of leadership in general and of President Bartlet in particular. In his match with Sam, Bartlet is the confident, clever diplomat and mentor, solving a potential crisis to everyone's satisfaction with subtlety and aplomb. In his match with Toby, he is off balance, uncomfortable, and vulnerable. Both portrayals are accurate.

Toby, temporarily serving as the mentor to Bartlet, reminds him of a story the first lady once told.

> TOBY: She said you were at a party once where you were bending the guy's ear. You were telling him that Ellie had mastered her multiplication tables and she was in third grade reading at a fifth-grade level and she loved books and she scored two goals for her soccer team the week before, you were going on and on. . . . And what made that story remarkable was that the party you were at was in Stockholm and the man you were talking to was King Gustav, who two hours earlier had given you the Nobel Prize in economics. (*laughs*) I mean, my god, you just won the Nobel Prize and all you wanted to talk about to the king of Sweden was Ellie's multiplication tables!
>
> BARTLET: (*approaches, irritably, to sit across from him*) What's your point?
>
> TOBY: You're a good father, you don't have to act like it. You're the president, you don't have to act like it. You're a good man, you don't have to act like it. You're not just folks, you're not plain-spoken. . . . Do not—do not—*do not* act like it!

Toby's perspective on his boss reinforces the Confucian ideal of centuries earlier, as well as Bartlet's advice to Sam. No one can be a leader without the help of others. Good leaders (and good principals) "listen to everybody and then call the play." Bartlet is brilliant *and* fallible, confident *and* insecure. He depends on his staff as much as they depend on him. As an individual, he is limited in what he can accomplish. But with the help of his team, he can "see the whole board."

SEEING THE WHOLE BOARD: SYSTEMS THINKING

"From a very early age," Peter Senge writes in *The Fifth Discipline*, "we are taught to break apart problems, to fragment the world."

This reflex makes complex tasks seem more approachable. But the truth is we all pay a price for deluding ourselves into thinking that everything can be broken down into cause and effect, accurately measured, and sufficiently addressed. Indeed, in the same way a reassembled broken mirror cannot yield an accurate reflection, "we can no longer see the consequences of our actions." Absent that capacity, "we lose our intrinsic sense of connection to a larger whole."[1]

In his book *Solving Tough Problems*, Adam Kahane postulates that one reason we oversimplify the problems we need to solve is because we fail to recognize the interplay of three different types of complexity: dynamic, generative, and social. "A problem has low *dynamic* complexity," Kahane writes, "if cause and effect are close together in space and time. In a car engine, for example, causes produce effects that are nearby, immediate, and obvious; and so, why an engine doesn't run can be understood and solved by testing and fixing one piece at a time."[2] By contrast, a problem has high dynamic complexity if cause and effect are far apart in space and time. This characterizes just about any major challenge faced by public schools today. Even the most intelligently crafted in-school interventions, for example, will never be able to fully overcome the myriad out-of-school factors impacting student achievement and engagement. Kahane says such problems "can only be understood systemically, taking account of the interrelationship among the pieces and the functioning of the system as a whole."

"A problem has low *generative* complexity," he continues, "if its future is familiar and predictable. In a traditional village, for example, the future simply replays the past, and so solutions and rules from the past will work in the future." By contrast, a problem has high generative complexity if its future is unfamiliar and unpredictable. Think again of the challenges faced by schools, which must depart from the traditional twentieth-century model of schooling to match the needs of students who are entering a radically different world than the one their parents entered. "Solutions to problems with high generative complexity cannot be calculated in advance, on paper, based on what has worked in the past, but have to be worked out as the situation unfolds.

"A problem has low *social* complexity if the people who are part of the problem have common assumptions, values, rationales, and objectives." This may have been true in the past, when one's neighborhood school was more likely to attract families of similar faiths, economic levels, and ethnicities. But a problem has high social complexity if the people who must solve it together see the world in very different ways. "Problems of high social complexity," Kahane says, "cannot be peacefully solved by authorities from on high; the people involved must participate in creating and implementing solutions."[3]

To create the cultural conditions that allow for such complexities to be uncovered and holistically addressed, Kahane, Senge, and others urge us to create "'learning organizations,' organizations where people continually expand their capacity to create the results they truly desire, where new and expansive patterns of thinking are nurtured, where collective aspiration is set free, and where people are continually learning how to learn together. . . . What fundamentally will distinguish learning organizations from traditional authoritarian 'controlling organizations,'" Senge explains, "will be the mastery of certain basic disciplines."[4]

In chapter 1, I introduced what I believe to be a foundational discipline of any member of a democratic learning community—the capacity to reflect personally, "see" our thinking, and develop the awareness we need to discover the inner place from which we operate. Now I want to introduce a second—what Senge and others call "systems thinking," and what President Bartlet calls "seeing the whole board."

As Senge explains it:

> A cloud masses, the sky darkens, leaves twist upward, and we know that it will rain. We also know that the storm runoff will feed into groundwater miles away, and the sky will clear by tomorrow. All these events are distant in time and space, and yet they are connected within the same pattern. Each has an influence on the rest, an influence that is usually hidden from view. You can only understand the system of a rainstorm by contemplating the whole, not any individual part of the pattern.[5]

The same principles hold true for the other networks we encounter in our lives:

> Business and other human endeavors are also systems. They, too, are bound by invisible fabrics of interrelated actions, which often take years to fully play out their effects on each other. Since we are part of that lacework ourselves, it's doubly hard to see the whole pattern of change. Instead, we tend to focus on snapshots of isolated parts of the system, and wonder why our deepest problems never seem to get solved. Systems thinking is a conceptual framework, a body of knowledge and tools that has been developed over the past fifty years to make the full patterns clearer, and to help us see how to change them effectively.[6]

Because it helps people see how personal actions contribute to the world around them, systems thinking is crucial to any healthy, evolving organization. "At the heart of a learning organization," Senge continues, "is a shift of mind—from seeing ourselves as separate from the world to connected to the world, from seeing problems as caused by someone or something 'out there' to seeing how our own actions create the problems we experience."[7]

The same ideas hold true for teachers, principals, and parents—our primary stewards for the institutions that should be the prototypical learning organizations. This doesn't mean educators and parents should necessarily all become experts in systems thinking (although it wouldn't hurt). But there are a few simple rules—based on systems principles—that can guide us. If heeded, these rules can help schools start to explore the underlying structures that shape individual actions, and begin to create the conditions that allow people to feel both more empowered by, and connected to, one another.

Don't Rely On Old Thinking to Solve New Problems

A good private-sector example of this idea at work is the story of the company that helped fuel my wife's and my *West Wing* habit—Netflix.

If you're not familiar with them yet, Netflix is the world's largest online movie rental service. Founded in 1998, the company revolutionized the way people rent a movie. Instead of going to the local video store, customers create their own online movie "queue." Netflix then mails these movies (or TV shows) directly to the customer. There are no late fees—just different pricing plans that determine how many DVDs you can have in your possession at one time. Once you've watched a DVD, just pack it up in the envelope Netflix provides and ship it back. As soon as Netflix receives it, the next selection on your list gets shipped. And so on.

In retrospect, the appeal of this business model is obvious. And yet Netflix was taking a huge risk by asking its customers to demonstrate a completely new behavior. This was not the same old way of thinking about how things are done. Send and receive movies by mail? Ridiculous. It will never work.

But it has worked. Concerns about customers keeping their videos forever were addressed by staged pricing plans. Worries about lag time in delivery were addressed by establishing more than 100 different shipping points located throughout the United States. And unlike major competitors like Blockbuster, Netflix has no store overhead costs to consider on its balance sheet. So while Blockbuster invested in larger and larger stores and inventories, Netflix read the tea leaves and steadily acquired its competitors' old customers.

That's seeing the whole board. And that's an example of not using yesterday's thinking to solve today's challenges.

This principle is equally important in the education community, especially at this point in history. As Princeton economist Allan Blinder notes, "It is clear that the U.S. and other rich nations will have to transform their educational systems so as to produce workers for the jobs that will actually exist in their societies."

Simply providing *more* education is probably a good thing on balance, especially if a more educated labor force is a more flexible labor force that can cope more readily with non-routine tasks and occupational change. But it is far from a panacea. . . . In the future, *how* we educate our children may prove to be more important than *how much* we educate them.[8]

If we agree with Blinder's assessment, we must acknowledge the pressing need to inject new ideas into an old system—a system so antediluvian that it is, remarkably, still based on the agrarian calendar. In short, we need Netflixian innovations in education, where we create new ways of seeing old structures and habits of being, not the Blockbuster approach, where we keep our heads down and continue doing what we've always done.

Unfortunately, our current public school system makes innovation difficult. As Harvard Business School professor Clayton Christensen explains in the book *Disrupting Class*, the U.S. education system is laced with four types of interdependencies: temporal ("You can't study this in ninth grade if you didn't cover it in the seventh."); lateral ("You can't teach certain foreign languages in more efficient ways because you'd have to change the way English grammar is taught."); physical ("You can't adopt project-based learning for young people because the layout of school buildings can't accommodate it."); and hierarchical ("You can't empower educators to innovate if federal, state, and local mandates are misaligned, and if the locus of power is remote from the schools themselves."). "Because there are so many points of interdependence within the public school system," Christensen says, "there are powerful economic forces in place to standardize both instruction and assessment despite what we know to be true—students learn in different ways. . . . The question now facing schools is this: Can the system of schooling designed to process groups of students in standardized ways in a monolithic instructional mode be adapted to handle differences in the way individual brains are wired for learning?"[9]

Apply this question to the elephant in the middle of any conversation about education for much of the past—the No Child Left Behind (NCLB) Act. Did the legislation reflect new thinking that will better prepare American children for the challenges (and jobs) of the twenty-first century? Or was it an attempt to use simple, linear thinking to solve complex, nonlinear problems?

In fact, NCLB is an archetypal system structure that arises whenever people treat symptoms of a problem and then become increasingly dependent on their own "symptomatic solutions." Rather than tackle the myriad issues that exacerbate the achievement gap between high-income and low-income students (an extremely worthy goal), what we've done instead is isolate one easily visible symptom of "school success"—in this case, student test scores and schoolwide annual yearly progress (AYP) reports—and then prescribe a cure: an increased emphasis on testing and accountability. But just as we must resist the urge to solve new problems with old thinking, we must beware of the symptomatic solution.

Beware the Symptomatic Solution

Senge calls this tendency "shifting the burden" and warns that not facing the real problem may cause it to get worse. Solutions that address only the symptoms of a problem, and not the fundamental cause(s), tend to have short-term benefits at best. "In the long-term," he says, "the problem resurfaces and there is increased pressure for a symptomatic response."[10] Meanwhile, the capacity to see and address more fundamental problems atrophies and we become unwittingly dependent on the "quick fix."

With some practice, it is possible to recognize shifting-the-burden structures and redirect our strategic responses. That's because shifting-the-burden structures are always made up of two balancing, or stabilizing, processes. One of these is the symptomatic solution; the other is the fundamental solution.

Both processes are always working to adjust or correct the same problem. For demonstration purposes, let's stick with the achievement gap in American public schools. The top circle of figure 2.1 represents the symptomatic solution—an increased national emphasis on testing. It may solve the problem, but only for a short time.

The bottom circle, which represents the more fundamental solution, has a delay built in, because its effects take longer to see. The fundamental solution is, however, the only enduring way to address the problem. Often the delay between the two solutions produces side effects—in this case, an increased dependence on testing as a form of measurement, more "drill and kill" instruction, and less emphasis on other subjects, besides reading and math, that go into a well-rounded education.

This process tends to reinforce, or amplify, the long-term challenges of the problem. Test scores may go up in the short term, but at the expense of teacher satisfaction and motivation—maybe even student curiosity, engagement, and passion for learning as well. Before we know it, schools are abandoning creative arts programs, devaluing innovation, and making the art of learning mirror Henry Ford's approach to the assembly of cars—regimented, consistent, predictable, repetitive.

To represent the way the side effects of a symptomatic solution can build and make matters worse over the long term, imagine a snowball rolling downhill. Meanwhile, the underlying problems—almost too complex to summarize, but I'll try by referring to the historic inequities of access and

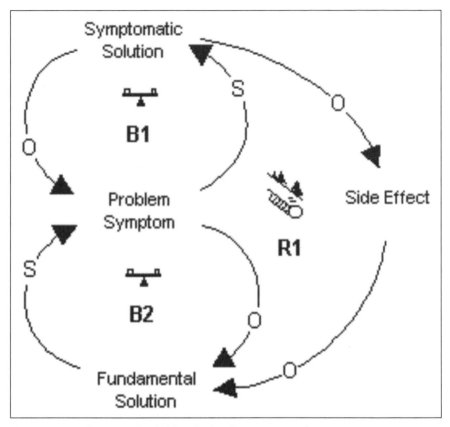

Figure 2.1. A diagram of a shifting-the-burden systems archetype.

opportunity that exist between people of different economic classes—remain unaddressed. Because of the snowball effect, the fundamental problems may even worsen. This, in turn, creates an even greater perceived need for the symptomatic solution. It creates an even greater discrepancy between the way high-income and low-income children are taught. It does nothing to address the ever-widening gap between rich and poor people in this country. And so on.

In technical terms this is known as a feedback loop, although here the word "feedback" means something very different from offering advice; it means a reciprocal flow of influence. The role of feedback reminds us that in a system every influence should be seen as both cause and effect.

There are two types of feedback loops to be aware of in systems thinking—positive (or amplifying) and negative (or regulatory). Positive feedback loops tend to amplify whatever change to the system has occurred. The shifting-the-burden dynamic I just outlined is an example of this process at work. In systems like these, small changes can have huge effects. The perturbation to the system snowballs. And the behavior that results generates either accelerating improvement or decline.

By contrast, regulatory feedback helps keep a system balanced once the course has been established. This type of feedback tends to operate whenever there is goal-oriented behavior. If the goal is one you like, regulatory feedback is a good thing. If it isn't, you'll be spinning your wheels unless you can change the goal or lessen its influence on the system.

Regulatory processes are everywhere. When you ride a bicycle and stay upright, that's a regulatory process. When you put on a sweater because you're cold, that's a regulatory process. And when you modify—either willingly or unwillingly—your Socratic teaching style to accommodate the larger goal of improved student test scores, that's a regulatory process as well.

What makes regulatory loops so important for our purposes is that there are explicit and implicit goals in organizations that shape how individual behavior is regulated.

Know Your Organization's Explicit and Implicit Goals

Knowing explicit (or visible) goals is the easy part. But the fact that implicit (or invisible) goals exist—and most organizations remain unaware of them—means we often fail to recognize when a balancing process, or system adjustment, is taking place.

If you're a teacher, imagine that your school principal has announced a new change initiative for the coming school year. An unwritten understanding of the faculty, however, is that the principal always falls in love with new ideas; this latest one, therefore, is generally seen as nothing more than the flavor of the month.

It's safe to say the change initiative will fail, no matter how much money is invested in new books, new training, or new mission statements. The system is maintaining its preferred state—in this case, the status quo. The principal is left scratching his head, unable to recognize that the resistance he's experiencing is a response by the system and a valuable insight into not just his own behavior but also the implicit goals of the community he serves.

Until implicit goals are recognized, any change or reform effort is essentially doomed to fail. Implicit goals are almost always a vivid reflection of the quality (or lack thereof) of relationships among the people who make up an organization. As Otto Scharmer explains, "In groups, organizations, and larger systems it is the structure of the relationship among individuals that—when changed—gives rise to different collective behavior patterns."[11]

If you know where to look, implicit goals are not hard to find. It's long been understood if you want to understand an organization's culture, just sit in on a staff meeting. This has been true for every school and organization I've worked with. A careful observer of a single faculty meeting would have been able to get a strong initial sense of the community's explicit and implicit goals—perhaps even the topics the group had silently agreed never to discuss.

As Senge writes, "Resistance to change is neither capricious nor mysterious. It almost always arises from threats to traditional norms and ways of doing things. Often these norms are woven into the fabric of established power relationships. The norm is entrenched because the distribution of authority and control is entrenched.

"Rather than pushing harder to overcome resistance to change, artful leaders discern the source of the resistance. They focus directly on the implicit norms and power relationships within which the norms are embedded."[12] And they expect delays to occur.

Expect Delays

In my first apartment in D.C., I endured an old, ineffective shower. The nozzle was too low for my head, forcing me to bend awkwardly to wash my hair. The handles were also slow to respond to my attempts to adjust the balance of hot and cold water. This usually resulted in me readjusting too quickly, only to find myself moments later getting scalded (or frozen).

I realize now I was experiencing what happens when people don't anticipate delays in a system. I desired the final result (the right temperature) quicker than the time it took to achieve it. Because it was nothing more than my morning ritual, this daily experience didn't extend beyond personal frustration. In a school, however, such delays can lead to generations of tinkering, false starts, and frustration.

Virtually any feedback process has some sort of delay. That's why, along with the two major feedback processes, delays provide the third building block for a language of systems thinking.

The key is to recognize a delay is taking place. When I adjusted the shower temperature but nothing happened, I perceived that my action had no effect. The more aggressively I tried to compensate, the longer it ultimately took me to reach the right balance of hot and cold water.

This dynamic provides one of the main lessons of regulatory feedback loops—the more drastic the intervention, the harder it is to reach your goal. *The harder you push, the harder the system pushes back.*

Whether finding the right balance in the shower or building the public will for a long-term view of education reform, understanding delays is a crucial aspect of any viable strategy to address fundamental problems. For the short term, these delays are easily ignored. Over the long haul, their consequences will always be brought to bear, no matter how hard we try to pretend otherwise.

It's the subtle lure of the Newtonian worldview. We desperately want to believe it is possible to find simple solutions to the complex problems we face and to neatly divide cause and effect. To improve student learning, the conventional wisdom goes, we must make schools (and teachers) more accountable to student test scores. To make schools safer, we must add more metal detectors.

The problem is that in a complex, interdependent system like a school, every influence is both cause and effect. Multiple-choice testing leads to multiple-choice teaching and a narrower and more test prep–centered pedagogy. The addition of metal detectors does nothing to improve—indeed, it may worsen—the quality of social trust in a school community. And so on. So how do we take this knowledge and become less imprisoned by the systems in which we operate?

Cure the System by Connecting it to More of Itself

These three key elements—regulatory and amplifying feedback loops and system delays—remind us we must recognize that short-term solutions usually come with a cost. The structures of which we are unaware hold us prisoner. And the longer we wait to address fundamental problems, the harder it will be to get the results we desire.

To understand and work with the school as a system, teachers, principals, and parents need to be able to observe it as a system. That means acquiring the ability to "see the whole board" by looking for the patterns at play in the school, not just the isolated incidents or data points.

Complicating matters is the fact that school systems are not always clearly defined by a core set of beliefs. What the central office believes may differ greatly from what different schools believe. Alternatively, individual schools may be internally divided by sharply divergent views about what needs to be done. In the absence of this alignment around a shared set of beliefs, schools often become balkanized and end up discouraging people from seeking out the very thing that would help the most—stronger relationships with one another.

In school or district environments such as these, many small systems develop under the artificial aegis of the "unified" school district. It is these actual systems—the clusters of relationships of like-minded individuals, and the implicit goals that drive them—that must be identified and worked with if any meaningful change is to occur.

Learning how to recognize systems, feedback processes, and delays is one step toward encouraging the creation of a healthy, self-aware learning organization. Anyone can start this by trying to identify archetypal structures at work in one's own school, and then strategizing about the best ways to address fundamental problems while taking implicit organizational goals into account. The Society for Organizational Learning (www.solonline.org/) provides consulting and training about systems thinking. And Peter Senge's *The Fifth Discipline* and Otto Scharmer's *Theory U* offer more detailed discussions than I have here.

Meg Wheatley sees an additional way.

> Once we recognize that organizations are webs there is much we can learn about organizational change just from contemplating spider webs. Most of us have had the experience of touching a spider web, feeling its resiliency, noticing how slight pressure in one area jiggles the entire web. If a web breaks and needs repair, the spider doesn't cut out a piece, terminate it, or tear the entire web apart and reorganize it. *She reweaves it*, using the silken relationships that are already there, creating stronger connections across the weakened spaces. The most profound strategy for changing a living network comes from biology. If a system is in trouble, it can be restored by connecting it to more of itself.[13]

To make stronger schools, therefore, we must create stronger relationships between people. To help my community become healthier, I must connect it to more of itself. And to bring about meaningful change, we must all strive to "help the system learn more about itself from itself."

This idea has major implications for how we define the ideal role of the principal in a school community. In the current national climate, if you ask a group of school principals to name the most important aspect of their job, the majority of responses will likely address the need to improve student achievement and learning. I don't disagree with the sentiment behind this answer at all—schools are first and foremost institutions of learning. But the generality of the answer connects back to the importance of "words, words, words," and the distinction I made in chapter 1 between vision and purpose.

If a principal's answer to the question is that her overarching goal is to improve student learning, she still hasn't told us (or herself) how she's going to do it. She's given us the abstract. But we need the concrete, and she does, too, if she hopes to lead with true clarity of purpose.

Clarity of purpose is one thing the great educator Myles Horton certainly had. Here's how he answered the question: "I think the role of an educator is to help people develop the capacity to make decisions and to take responsibility [for their own actions]."[14]

The National Association of Secondary School Principals (NASSP) is of a similar mind. Among its seven cornerstone strategies to improve student performance are these two: "Increase the quantity and improve the quality of interactions between students, teachers and other school personnel," and "Allow for meaningful involvement in decision-making by students, teachers, family members, and the community."[15]

So what does this all mean?

To "suit the word to the action, and the action to the word," we must develop the capacity to describe our shared purpose, simply and clearly. We must understand not just our shared purpose but also our own personal vision. We must see the patterns that shape our behavior. We must have the courage to become more reflective and think in new ways about the problems we face. We must resist quick fixes. And those of us in positions of leadership must remember that our role is to serve as translators, not creators, of people's dreams.

CONNECT—FIVE THINGS YOU CAN DO

Read *Theory U*

Across all fields, top-down management models are increasingly out of step with the personal needs of people and the optimal conditions for productivity. This has created a pressing need for new methods of mobilizing individual and collective intelligence in the service of social change.

Otto Scharmer's book *Theory U* is a major contribution to this search. The book presents a range of principles and practices for developing the capacity for innovative leadership. The principles of *Theory U* can help school leaders break through past unproductive patterns of behavior that recycle ineffective patterns of decision making.

Check Out the Creative Learning Exchange

The mission of the Creative Learning Exchange (www.clexchange.org) is to "develop Systems Citizens in K–12 education who use systems thinking and system dynamics to meet the interconnected challenges that face them at personal, community, and global levels." CLE has useful resources, a conference, a newsletter, and all sorts of ideas for people interested in strengthening systems thinking knowledge in a school.

Take a Systems Thinking Workshop

One of the best ways to become more comfortable with the change process is to develop the capacity to see and diagnose problems and challenges more systemically.

To help educators acquire these skills, the Waters Foundation was founded to "increase the capacity of educators to deliver student academic and lifetime benefits through the effective application of systems thinking concepts, habits and tools in classroom instruction and school improvement."

To find classroom lessons, schedule a workshop, or access its list of resources, visit www.watersfoundation.org.

Attend a Pegasus Conference

Since 1989, Pegasus Communications has tried to help individuals, teams, and organizations thrive in an increasingly complex world. At Pegasus's annual Systems Thinking in Action Conference, leading theorists and practitioners from around the world meet to explore new concepts, build (and apply) their skills, and share knowledge about systems thinking and organizational change.

To learn more about the Pegasus Conference, visit www.pegasuscom.com.

Spend a Day in a Different School (or Shadow a Colleague)

Sometimes, all it takes to begin seeing things differently is a subtle shift in our environment. A great way to do this is by spending a professional development day in a neighboring school—or by closely shadowing a colleague in your own school—and observing closely what you see.

Some structured debriefing may make the experience even more useful. Here are a few sample questions you might consider:

- What struck me (or surprised me) the most? Why did this stand out?
- With what did I connect most personally? Why did this touch me?
- If the shared culture of the school I visited was a living thing, what would it look, feel, and act like?
- If that living thing could talk, what would it say to us?
- If it could develop, what would it want to morph into next?
- What aspects of the culture (good and bad) are allowing this "living thing" to thrive?
- What aspects (good or bad) are hindering its further development?
- If the shared culture of my own school was a living thing, how would it resemble what I just described? How is it different?

- Based on my answers to the above questions, what are the major implications I must confront before moving forward?

NOTES

1. Peter Senge, *The Fifth Discipline* (New York & London: Doubleday, 1990, 2006), 3.

2. Adam Kahane, *Solving Tough Problems* (San Francisco: Berrett-Kohler, 2004, 2007), 31.

3. Ibid.

4. Senge, *The Fifth Discipline*, 5.

5. Senge, *The Fifth Discipline*, 6.

6. Senge, *The Fifth Discipline*, 7.

7. Senge, *The Fifth Discipline*, 12.

8. Cited in Thomas Friedman, *The World is Flat* (New York: Farrar, Giroux & Strauss, 2005, 2006), 302.

9. Clayton M. Christensen et al., *Disrupting Class: How Disruptive Innovation Will Change the Way the World Learns* (New York: McGraw Hill, 2008), 34, 35.

10. Senge, *The Fifth Discipline*, 103.

11. C. Otto Scharmer, *Theory U: Leading From the Future as it Emerges* (Cambridge, MA: SOL, 2007), 228.

12. Senge, *The Fifth Discipline*, 88.

13. Margaret Wheatley, *Leadership and the New Science* (San Francisco: Berrett-Kohler, 2006), 145.

14. Myles Horton and Paolo Freire, *We Make the Road by Walking*, eds. Brenda Bell, John Gaventa, and John Peters (Philadelphia: Temple University Press, 1990), 125.

15. NASSP, *Breaking Ranks II: Strategies for Leading High School Reform* (Reston, VA: NASSP, 2004), 6.

Chapter Three

Create
(or, recognize that "people
support only what they create")

*During a one-day celebration, the quad of Amherst College became a new physical,
cultural, and psychological landscape as the community added
the first layer of color to the portraits.*

> Disciplined people who engage in disciplined thought and take disciplined action—operating with freedom within a framework of responsibilities—this is the cornerstone of a culture that creates greatness.
>
> —Jim Collins

Here's what most of my professional development experiences have felt like:

I'm attending a meeting with a large group of colleagues. Shortly after it begins, we're broken up into smaller groups and given a task that is in some way related to the larger goal of the meeting. Our instructions are to discuss the assigned issue with our smaller group and then report out what we learn. Once the conversation begins, a few voices tend to dominate. One dutiful person (please, not me) assumes the responsibility of taking notes.

After the allotted period of time, our group summarizes its conversation for the whole group. As we do, the facilitator takes notes on a flipchart. After each group has reported out, a master list is created. The facilitator takes this list and posts it somewhere on the wall.

Sound familiar? Almost every professional has had the experience of participating in this sort of meeting—and reviewing a master list that fails to capture the collective wisdom and energy of the group.

Now, imagine the same sort of meeting being conducted in a slightly different way.

We've been called together to discuss how to create a healthier, more democratic, and inclusive climate at our school. The facilitator does not leave us to our own devices when we break into smaller groups; she uses a CFG dialogue protocol to guarantee equity of airtime and provoke more authentic responses.

The protocol, "Attributes of a Learning Community" (see table 3.1), begins with each person spending five minutes thinking and writing about the best learning community they have ever experienced. It may be a school, a church, or a summer camp. The location doesn't matter, or the age at which the person experienced it—only that it was deeply meaningful and real learning occurred.

In smaller groups, each person shares his or her personal story. The rest of the group listens actively for key attributes that emerge. The teams are reminded that the purpose is not to whittle away valuable staff time telling stories but to use personal narratives as a powerful source of data that can shape both personal approaches to teaching and future decisions about school priorities. Left unsaid is the additional bonus that, along the way, each participant will gain new insights about their colleagues.

Once everyone has a chance to tell their story, the central facilitator asks each group to reflect on their list and come up with the three to five most

Table 3.1   Attributes of a Learning Community

Purpose: To establish the basic attributes of transformational learning communities through real participant experiences. The attributes can then become goals and/or guidelines for evaluating progress as a new learning community develops.

Time: One hour

Steps:

1. The group identifies a timekeeper.
2. Participants write silently about their most meaningful, personal experience in a learning community. It could be a club, a church group, a school experience, a course, a support group, etc. The only criteria are that it was a positive experience and real learning occurred. (4 min)
3. In groups of three to five, participants share their stories with one another. As each story is told, the rest of the group listens actively and takes notes on what they hear. (4 min per story)
4. After the story is finished, the group asks clarifying questions of the presenter. *These are purely informational,* in order to ensure that the group understands the story well enough to identify what attributes made it such a successful experience. (3 min)
5. After clarifying questions, the group discusses the presenter's story and clarifies which attributes emerged and were most resonant. *The group does this as though the presenter is no longer in the room. She is spoken about in the third person.* (3 min)
6. The group checks in with the presenter—who has magically reappeared—to confirm that their list of attributes is the right list. (1 min)
7. Rinse. Repeat.

important attributes. These do not need to be the attributes that show up most often in the stories—a great attribute may have surfaced just once. These characteristics are shared with the whole group. As this is done, the facilitator creates a central list on a flipchart, which she posts on a wall and then asks the participants to reflect on its contents.

Although the two approaches are similar, they produce vastly different results. In the first scenario, the effort to encourage broad participation falls flat, whereas the second process results in a list people are more likely to find meaningful.

Why is the second method more effective? According to James Zull, the author of *The Art of Changing the Brain*, it has to do with how the different processes apply what we know about cognitive science. "Above all," Zull writes, "the brain wants *survival*. To survive we must be in control, or believe that we are. . . . And we survive by thinking, planning and deciding."[1]

The part of the brain that controls how we think, plan, and decide is called the neocortex, so named because, in evolutionary terms at least, it hasn't been in use that long. In fact, although we are born with the capacity for emotions like fear and pleasure, we still aren't born knowing what to fear or what gives us pleasure.

Learning what does and doesn't work for us personally is essential for survival. "We might say that our best chance to help another person learn is to find out what they want, what they care about."[2] When we ground these discoveries in personal experience, we give them a feel that makes us more likely to trust the sensory input from the experience itself.

Stories are particularly effective, Zull reports, because they engage all parts of the brain. "We remember by connecting things with our stories, we create by connecting our stories together in unique and memorable ways, and we act out our stories together in our behaviors."[3]

In other words, whereas one scenario leaves the role of personal stories and equal participation to chance, the other is structured to ensure that everyone gets a say and all contributions are anchored in personal memories.

The more one learns about cognitive science and organizational theory, the more one realizes how slight nuances in structure and strategy can make the difference between a productive meeting and a wasted afternoon. Simply put, we have no choice but to invite people to participate in the decisions that shape their lives.

It's not about "buy in," either—despite the popularity of the term. If anything, the term itself is a reminder of why it's so important we recognize how the words we choose shape our interpretations of what is and isn't necessary. Are we trying to sell someone on someone else's idea or program? If so, the most we can likely hope for is extrinsic motivation, otherwise known as compliance. Or are we trying to spark a more intrinsic type of motivation—a commitment—that helps a group of people achieve greater clarity about what needs to be done to support student learning?

People will insist on the freedom to participate, whether we ask them or not. "For the past fifty years," Meg Wheatley writes, "a great bit of wisdom has circulated in the field of organizational behavior: People support what they create."[4] Wheatley believes the maxim needs to be slightly restated: People support only what they create.

Remembering this fundamental principle of human learning and behavior isn't just a good strategy for leadership; it's the central principle on which this nation was founded. The First Amendment enshrines this principle in our body of laws by protecting the right of the people to speak out on all matters of conscience and ensure their voices are heard. Thomas Jefferson believed our founding documents didn't go far enough; in an 1816 letter, he proposed a constitutional amendment to facilitate grassroots democracy, suggesting that "counties be divided into wards of such size that every citizen can attend, when called on, and act in person."[5]

Jefferson believed that "making every citizen an acting member of the government, and in the offices nearest and most interesting to him, will attach him by his strongest feelings to the independence of his country, and its republican constitution."[6] Years later, buoyed by neurological research, Zull contends something similar. And the same spirit is found in the recommendations of top private sector consultants, such as Harvard professor John Kotter. "Considerable research," he reported in a *Harvard Business Review* article, "has demonstrated that, in general, participation leads to commitment, not merely compliance."[7]

IDENTIFYING THE CHARACTERISTICS OF LIVING SYSTEMS

Before any of us will be willing to change anything, we must first believe the changes will be meaningful to us. Anyone that has tried and failed to convince other people about an idea they believed to be particularly compelling knows this intuitively. As Wheatley explains, "Our colleagues are failing to respond because they don't share our sense that this is meaningful. *This is a failure to find shared significance, not a failure to communicate.* They have exercised their freedom and chosen not to be disturbed."[8]

Usually, we react negatively when we encounter this "lack of understanding" or "inability to follow basic orders," especially when it occurs in our professional environments, and especially when we're the boss. And yet this is basic human behavior—the desire for the freedom to choose. It's what Hamlet was denied by the social mores that constrained him. It's certainly what every student is striving for—consciously or unconsciously. And it's what led the physicist and systems theorist Fritjof Capra to propose three basic characteristics of living systems: they constantly create and recreate themselves; they constantly reorganize themselves in unpredictable ways; and they constantly demonstrate their awareness by the way they interact with their environment.[9]

Although Capra's list stems from his observations across the fields of physics, chemistry, and biology, these three characteristics are highly relevant for any organizational leader. The symptoms of these factors at work, however, are often ignored or disregarded.

A former school leader of mine provides a useful example. Over the summer, she decided the community would spend several days at the start of the year talking about ethics. The objective of the conversations was to produce a new set of shared ethics for the school that would apply to both adults and students. It was a worthy idea, and she tried to make the process as collaborative as possible—different classrooms would have simultaneous conversations, and the final list would be an amalgam of the best ideas.

However, because the adults felt the whole process had been sprung upon them, no one felt any real investment in the work—even though, under different circumstances, it wouldn't have been difficult to get the faculty to agree that a shared list of ethics was something that might help the school.

You can guess how it went from there. The teachers facilitating the classroom conversations weren't interested in taking the time to make those conversations meaningful. The students intuited from their teachers' words and actions that this was not something worth taking seriously. And the final list of ethics, widely posted, never became a living document at the school.

I imagine my former boss wondering afterward why her plan hadn't taken hold in the way she had envisioned. At the time, I remember feeling relieved that it was over so I, like the other teachers, could "go back to what we normally do." I now see that the reason for her failure was simple—people only support what they create.

Once we know this explicitly, those of us who are school leaders must realize the art of becoming a more democratic learning community cannot look like the solitary painting of one person, nor can the work come with a clear, predetermined set of action steps and answers.

Leaders don't need to have all the answers. In a healthy organizational culture with a high degree of generative complexity, you can't possibly know them all. The answers will come from the people—the administration, the community, the faculty, the parents, and the students. And the chief role of the leader is to create the conditions that will support that process of co-creation. As President Bartlet understood, "You listen to everybody and then you call the play."

The biologist Francisco Varela has offered a new definition in his field that fits equally well here. An organization's intelligence, he explains, comes less from its ability to solve problems, and more from the ability of its members to co-create a world whose significance is shared. In other words, everyone needs to feel that what is taking place is meaningful—even as they have different perspectives. Fellow scientist Fritjof Capra agrees: "In recent years, biologists and ecologists have begun to shift their metaphors from hierarchies to networks (see table 3.2) and have come to realize that partnership—the tendency to associate, establish links, cooperate, and maintain symbiotic relationships—is one of the hallmarks of life."[10]

In *The Right to Learn*, Stanford University professor Linda Darling-Hammond underscores Varela's and Capra's observations. Referencing an eight-year research study, Darling-Hammond reports

Table 3.2   Principles of Ecology[1]

Networks
At all scales of nature, we find living systems nesting within other living systems—
networks within networks. Their boundaries are not boundaries of separation but
boundaries of identity. All living systems communicate with one another and share
resources across their boundaries.

Cycles
All living organisms must feed on continual flows of matter and energy from their
environment to stay alive, and all living organisms continually produce waste.
However, an ecosystem generates no net waste, one specie's waste being another
specie's food. Thus, matter cycles continually through the web of life.

Solar Energy
Solar energy, transformed into chemical energy by the photosynthesis of green plants,
drives ecological cycles.

Partnership
The exchanges of energy and resources in an ecosystem are sustained by pervasive
cooperation. Life did not take over the planet by combat but by cooperation,
partnership, and networking.

Diversity
Ecosystems achieve stability and resilience through the richness and complexity of their
ecological webs. The greater their biodiversity, the more resilient they will be.

Dynamic Balance
An ecosystem is a flexible, ever-fluctuating network. Its flexibility is a consequence of
multiple feedback loops that keep the system in a state of dynamic balance. No single
variable is maximized; all variables fluctuate around their optimal values.

1. Fritjof Capra, *The Hidden Connections: Integrating the Biological, Cognitive and Social Dimensions of Life Into A Science of Sustainability* (New York: Doubleday, 2002), 231.

> The most successful schools were distinguished by the process of inquiry staff undertook together rather than by the content of the particular reforms they developed. Their success came from their search for shared goals, which they used to guide curriculum and organizational decisions. Teachers and administrators reported that it was the collective thinking stimulated by this process that engendered the vitality, willingness to change, and conviction to continue that changed the life of their school.[11]

Despite such studies, the principle of co-creation rarely appears in school mission statements. In one school where I worked, I never even knew what the mission statement was.

By contrast, consider the focus of a small public school in New Hampshire called Monadnock Community Connections School—or MC[2] for short (see chapter 8). Their mission statement was clearly written with Varela's definition of organizational intelligence in mind: "Empowering each individual with the knowledge and skills to use his/her unique voice effectively and with integrity in co-creating our common public world."

Implicit in the MC^2 mission statement is the idea that no school becomes more democratic by fiat. As educational scholar John Goodlad observed, following his massive comprehensive study of schooling in America, "Schools will improve slowly, if at all, if reforms are thrust upon them. Rather, the approach having most promise is one that will seek to cultivate the capacity of schools to deal with their own problems, to become largely self-renewing."[12] Myles Horton agrees: "If you believe in democracy, which I do, you have to believe that people have the capacity within themselves to develop the ability to govern themselves."[13] And as Wheatley writes, "Everyone requires the freedom to author their own life. . . . We're seeing people exercising their inalienable freedom to create themselves. They take *our* work and recreate it as *their* work. And this process of recreation can't be stopped without deadening that person."[14]

Any intention to create a more inclusive school culture must therefore begin with the recognition that schools are not machines; they are complex, living systems. No one can be forced to change, and no two people see the world the same way. All change must therefore begin with a change in beliefs and assumptions and a shift in the inner place from which we operate.

BUILDING A SHARED VISION

In chapter 1, I talked about the importance of making sense of our visions for the work we do. In this section, I want to underscore a key distinction—for meaningful change to occur, the organization's shared vision should not be seen as the property of any one person.

At first blush, these two ideas may seem contradictory. But there is a progression at work here, and it's not strictly linear. Our professional relationships, after all, will always cycle back and influence our personal behavior and overall sense of self.

Nonetheless, the progression toward a democratic approach to work assumes that before any of us can create truly healthy relationships with our colleagues, we must first understand ourselves better. That process begins by developing a greater familiarity with the memories, ideas, and challenges that motivate us as individuals. It continues as we cultivate relationships with those around us—relationships that become, one hopes, less colored by our personal insecurities and defenses. And it culminates in the reward of a co-created organizational culture whereby our internal passions, our external actions, and our shared sense of purpose are more effectively aligned.

Organizational leaders, intent on cultivating a shared vision for their school, must therefore continually encourage people to develop and define their own personal visions. The contrast between these individual visions (what people want and need from their professional lives) and collective goals (where the school stands in relation to these aggregate wants and needs) will provide the ongoing source of creative tension, or "civil friction," that helps drive each person's sense of motivation, purpose, and need. What is likely to emerge over time is a new organizational skill—the capacity to feel comfortable with the discomfort of respectfully competing ideas.

Again, we see a direct parallel to the First Amendment and the role it plays, theoretically at least, in American society. In the same way a good school leader encourages his staff to raise new ideas and respectfully question how to make the organization better, America's founders guaranteed the right of all Americans to voice their opinions without fear in the public square, in the interest of inviting the civil friction that helps give birth to all genuine dialogue and innovative thinking.

In schools, organizations, and societies, this arrangement doesn't work unless individual citizens are willing to look beyond just their individual rights. As the great American judge Learned Hand said in a 1944 speech, the spirit of liberty is the spirit which is not too sure that it is right.

It is essential in a democratic learning community that we assume responsibility for not just our own ideas but also the ideas of our colleagues—especially those with whom we most deeply disagree—and that we always strive to debate our differences with respect. The conflicts we work out in the public square may be different from the debates we have in our public schools, but the fundamental principle in both arenas is the same—in a community of free people, the privilege of sharing one's opinion must be accompanied by the responsibility of honoring that same privilege in others and a shared commitment to give voice to our ideas in a spirit of respectful inquiry and exchange.

The central organizational challenge, once again, is striking that balance between individual freedom and group structure: Freedom for all to express their opinions, balanced by a shared framework of rules and expectations that clarify what the community values and what it will and will not accept.

In his 1983 book *How to Speak, How to Listen*, Mortimer Adler described the role public education has in ensuring this balance:

The enforcement of [the First Amendment] may guarantee that public discussion of public issues goes on unfettered, but it does not and cannot ensure that the discussion is as good as it should be, either by the people's representatives in Congress or by the people themselves when they assemble for the purpose of political discussion. This cannot be secured by any constitutional enactment or any act of government. Improvement in the quality of public discussion and political debate can be achieved only by improvement in the quality of the schooling that the people as a whole receive.[15]

To fully participate in the world around us, we need to learn more than the history of free speech or individual rights; we need to practice those rights —thoughtfully and deliberately. We should actively do so in our schools, which are smaller experiments of this basic American principle. Otherwise, all we're doing is asking future generations of Americans to "buy into" someone else's vision. In such a situation, the best we can hope for is compliance. To become a transformational society—or, more locally, a transformational school—we must strive for commitment.

The role of the principal is crucial if this sort of progression is to become possible in a school. She sets the tone that will either encourage or discourage a climate of personal exploration and strong, open relationships. Unless she is willing to continually share her personal vision and recognize that her position does not entitle her ideas to become the "organizational vision" by default, it is unlikely her staff will feel comfortable enough to contribute their ideas openly and consistently.

This may be the hardest lesson for a leader to apply consistently: There is no one thing you can do to get people to feel committed.

To really commit to an idea, we must feel we are free to decide whether or not the idea is the right one. Transformational leaders create the climate whereby we feel both free and secure to make the choices that are meaningful to us and to the group. Although a democratic school climate cannot, by itself, cause people to feel more committed to each other, it does make such an ethic of commitment more likely. As Myles Horton observed, "When you provide people with opportunities to learn for themselves by making decisions, there are two concepts that are central: social equality and freedom of speech. . . . If we are to have a democratic society, people must find or invent new channels through which decisions can be made. Given genuine decision-making powers, people will not only learn rapidly to make socially useful decisions, but they will also assume responsibility for carrying out decisions based on their collective judgment."[16]

Many of us have come to feel that this original promise of democracy is something that rarely takes root in real life. Horton continues:

The problem is not that people will make irresponsible or wrong decisions. It is, rather, to convince people who have been ignored or excluded in the past that their involvement will have meaning and that their ideas will be respected.

The danger is not too much, but too little participation. Popular education should give people experience in making decisions. Many take it for granted that people can make decisions, but actually the majority of us are not allowed to make decisions about most of the things that are important.[17]

As Yale psychology professor James Comer points out, inviting people to be cocreators of their school involves more than simply saying, "You are welcome," or "Y'all come." Comer's approach to whole-school improvement, the School Development Program (SDP), is therefore centered on creating a school climate "that enables doubting parents to experience respect and comfort, to be supported, to get involved and be supportive of the school, and to help create the conditions that enable their children to succeed—reinforcing parental participation."[18]

What makes the Comer process effective is its ability to provide schools with a common language ("words, words, words") to talk about children and their behavior. And what defines transformational leaders is their willingness to ask questions (see table 3.3) and be fully present to hear—and act on—the answers they receive.

Table 3.3   Key Questions to Consider in a School Community

For Parents	For Students	For Staff	For the Community
What do you want for your children as adults?	What issues or problems do you feel are most important for the school and community to address?	What assumptions do we make about our school that no longer work? What new assumptions do we need to generate?	Can our graduates teach themselves? Do they have the tools they need to be self-directed lifelong learners?
What kinds of experiences will they need to be able to achieve these goals?	What you are passionate about? What do you do well? In what ways do you struggle?	What have we informally agreed never to talk about?	Are our graduates decent people? Has the school paid enough attention to helping its students acquire civil character?
How can we begin to prepare them to achieve these goals while they are still in school?	If there was one thing you wanted to be sure to learn before graduating, what would it be?	Of all the things we can do with our time together, what must we do?	Can our graduates use the skills in the different disciplines (e.g., science history, etc.) to see the world more effectively?

If you're unsure where to start, you might begin by asking the broadest number of people possible (or, if necessary initially, some pilot group) to spend a few minutes imagining, and then describing, their school as an archetypal family. What are the characteristics of this family? Are the parents divorced or married? How many children does this family have? What are their greatest struggles? Do the students from this family gravitate more toward a particular interest in school, say athletics? What are the characteristics of this young person's home life? Is he known as a hard worker? What are this individual's strengths and weaknesses, both as a student and as a person? What does he still need? What does his family need?

Structuring the exercise this way tends to open up people's ability to think creatively, resulting in new connections and ways of seeing a school's strongest inclinations that didn't previously exist. This may partly be a result of how the imaginative process engages the brain differently. As James Zull explains, "Metaphors are sets of neuronal networks that possess specific physical relationships to each other and thus embody the concept of the relationship itself."[19]

Once every person has a chance to describe their family's profile, the group spends a few minutes reflecting on which attributes were heard most often. What tends to emerge is a clearer collective picture of both the community and the school culture, as embodied by the aggregate description of an archetypal family and young person who reflect that culture—in both positive and negative ways.

Next, ask everyone to spend a few minutes describing the ideal graduate of their school. What does this person understand about herself and the world? What skills can she demonstrate and perform? What types of behaviors does she engage in on a daily basis? Once everyone has shared their vision, the group can again reflect on which attributes emerge as the most resonant.

The final step is to compare the two descriptions. In a perfectly aligned world they will be the same. Don't be upset when they aren't; the objective is to generate valuable data that can guide future decisions as a school community. Indeed, the question then becomes, quite clearly, "What do we need to do to eliminate the discrepancy between where our children are and where we want them to be?"

"MEANING BEHAVES LIKE ENERGY"

The school-as-a-family exercise is likely to provide a powerful source of motivation because, as Meg Wheatley points out:

> A living network will only transmit what it decides is meaningful. Meaning behaves like energy. It doesn't behave in mechanistic ways. Therefore, we can

abandon many of our mechanistic assumptions about what is required for organizational change. We don't have to achieve "critical mass"; we don't need programs that "roll out" (or over) the entire organization; we don't need to train every individual or part; we can stop obsessing if we don't get the support of the top of the organization. Instead, we can work locally, finding the ideas and processes that are meaningful in one area of the system. If we succeed in generating energy in one area, we can watch how our other networks choose to notice what we're doing. Who takes notice? Where have our ideas traveled in the organizational web? If we ask these questions, we learn who might be ready to take up this work next.[20]

I believe this insight has profound implications for how we structure group conversations, events, and planning sessions. Instead of getting people to "buy into" something, we should be creating opportunities for people to discover what matters to them and then follow the meaning. We should evoke contribution through freedom, not conformity. Or, as leadership consultant Myron Rogers puts it, start anywhere and follow it everywhere.

Malcolm Gladwell supports this thesis in his best-selling book, *The Tipping Point*. "Ideas and products and messages and behaviors spread just like viruses do," he explains. "When we're trying to make an idea or attitude or product tip, we're trying to change our audience in some small yet critical respect: we're trying to infect them, sweep them up in our epidemic, convert them from hostility to acceptance."[21]

Central to the process of having ideas tip is giving people the space to make the ideas their own. As Chip and Dan Heath explain in *Made to Stick: Why Some Ideas Survive and Others Die*:

> In making ideas stick, the audience gets a vote. The audience may change the meaning of your idea. . . . The audience may actually improve your idea. . . . Or the audience may retain some of your ideas and jettison others. . . . [But] if the world takes our ideas and changes them—or accepts some and discards others—all we need to decide is whether the mutated versions are still core. If they are, then we should humbly accept the audience's judgment.[22]

If you extend this idea to the Newtonian worldview, you're likely to feel exhausted. In the fragmentary world of cause and effect, the only way you get something to move is by expending personal energy. This is why so many change initiatives feel like they take valuable energy away from us.

If you view this same principle through the lens of quantum theory, a very different picture emerges. Quantum scientists no longer see space as a giant, empty void, but as a rich network of fields—invisible, nonmaterial substances that comprise the basic substance of the universe.

The scientific concept of fields encourages us to think similarly of our own spaces. All around us, there are both material and nonmaterial forces at play. In the field world, the potential for influence exists wherever two energies meet.

What does this look like when it gets played out in a school? To answer that question, it may help to go back to my opening description of a group meeting.

Think about the second example—the one where the group has produced a list it finds meaningful. What usually happens next in this situation? If you imagine a subsequent meeting where individuals take their copy of the list back and share it with other, larger groups, you're on the right track.

This happens repeatedly; when we experience something that is meaningful, we want to share it with others. We may even feel we've found the answer everyone else has been looking for. "We're about to solve the problem," we think. "Everyone will be so grateful."

Now imagine you're the facilitator and you can go back in time. You see people start to write down the list the group has just created. You know their intention is to take the list (e.g., The Answer) back to some other group of people and offer it as a solution of sorts. You also know this will result in more spinning wheels and frustration.

You decide to do something drastic. You rip the list up before anyone can finish writing it down. Gasps ring out from the group. "What are you doing?" they cry. "We need that list!"

Do you see what your answer should be?

It's not the list that's meaningful. It's the process by which this or any group of people co-creates the list. Bring *that* back. And follow the meaning.

CREATE—FIVE THINGS YOU CAN DO

Read *How People Learn*

How People Learn: Brain, Mind, Experience and School shares the findings of a two-year study conducted by the Committee on Developments in the Science of Learning.[23] In the book, a diverse coalition of scholars report that "the revolution in the study of the mind that has occurred in the last three or four decades has important implications for education." In particular, the book recommends teaching practices that "help people take control of their own learning" and encourages learners to "focus on sense-making, self-assessment, and reflection on what worked and what needs improving." Further echoing the ideas of this chapter, the scholars report that "learners of all ages are more motivated when they see the usefulness of what they are learning and when they can use that information to do something that has an impact on others—especially their local community."

Learn How to Conduct a Socratic Seminar

The National Paideia Center (www.paideia.org) serves as a source of information, inspiration, and training for those who are dedicated to transforming whole schools into activist learning communities based on the Paideia philosophy. The Paideia Center's professional development offerings help educators cultivate active learning environments and teach students how to think. Participants learn how to use a blend of three different types of instruction to enhance the literacy, problem-solving, and thinking skills of all students.

Identify the Attributes of a Learning Community

The National School Reform Faculty's Attributes of a Learning Community protocol is a group exercise that begins with each participant spending five minutes thinking and writing about the best learning community they have ever experienced. It may be a school, a church, or a summer camp. The location doesn't matter, or the age at which the person experienced it—only that it was deeply meaningful and real learning occurred.

In smaller groups, each person then shares his or her personal story. The rest of the group listens actively for key attributes that emerge. Once everyone has a chance to tell their story, a central facilitator asks each group to reflect on their list and come up with the three to five most important attributes. These do not need to be the attributes that show up most often in the stories—a great attribute may have surfaced just once. Each list is then shared with the whole group.

The resulting list of attributes, grounded in meaningful personal experiences, should help your group ground its work going forward in two key areas: First, the ways in which your shared culture is already aligned to reflect what the community knows to be a powerful learning environment; and second, the areas in which it must improve.

To download a PDF of the Attributes protocol, visit www.nsrfharmony.org. To share your story, and to hear the stories of others, visit www.rethinklearningnow. com.

Loosen Your Grip on Decision Making

The essence of cocreating a learning environment is making sure space exists for people to share their ideas and spur each other's thinking. This is why "buy in" is a misleading phrase—the only time we need to people to "buy in" is when it's our idea that needs their support.

If you're the person calling together a group to do collaborative work, try loosening your grip on what the end result needs to look like. This doesn't mean ceding your initial ideas entirely. It does, however, mean painting a picture for the group that is intentionally incomplete. Provide broad brush strokes and leave ample room for people to fill in the remaining blank space on the canvas. Whatever emerges will truly reflect the collective wisdom of the group.

Track the Aspirations of Your Students

What accounts for the difference between a student who talks about goals and one who actually reaches them? What makes the difference between a student who works hard at everyday tasks, and one whose hard work leads to a promising future?

The difference, according to the Quaglia Institute for Student Aspirations (QISA), is in the student's aspirations—his or her ability to set goals and think about the future while being inspired in the present to reach those goals.

In order to help schools and educators foster a learning culture that heightens student aspirations, QISA has developed the Aspirations Profile, which presents a visual model of the behaviors that support and hinder success.

To learn more about QISA and its work helping K–12 schools put into practice (and assess) the conditions that foster student aspirations, visit www. qisa.org.

NOTES

1. James E. Zull, *The Art of Changing the Brain* (Sterling, VA: Stylus Publishing, 2002), 48–49.

2. Ibid., 48.

3. Ibid., 228.

4. Margaret Wheatley, *Leadership and the New Science* (San Francisco: Berrett-Kohler, 2006), 89.

5. Cited in Robert Putnam, *Bowling Alone* (New York: Simon & Schuster, 2000), 336.

6. Ibid.

7. John P. Kotter and Leonard A. Schlesinger, "Choosing Strategies for Change," *Harvard Business Review* (March–April 1979): p. 7.

8. Wheatley, *Leadership and the New Science*, 88.

9. See, generally, Fritjof Capra, *The Hidden Connections: Integrating the Biolog-*

ical, Cognitive and Social Dimensions of Life Into A Science of Sustainability (New York: Doubleday, 2002).

10. Capra, *Hidden Connections*, 114.

11. Linda Darling-Hammond, *The Right to Learn* (San Francisco: Jossey-Bass, 1997), 215.

12. John Goodlad, *A Place Called School* (New York: McGraw Hill, 2004, 1984), 31.

13. Myles Horton, *The Long Haul* (New York & London: Teacher's College Press, 1998), 131.

14. Wheatley, *Leadership and the New Science*, 86–87.

15. Mortimer J. Adler, *How to Speak, How to Listen* (New York: Touchstone, 1983).

16. Horton, *The Long Haul*, 134, 137.

17. Ibid.

18. James P. Comer, *Leave No Child Behind* (New Haven & London: Yale University Press, 2004), 142.

19. Zull, *Art of Changing*, 127.

20. Margaret J. Wheatley, *Finding Our Way: Leadership for an Uncertain Time* (San Francisco: Berrett-Koehler Publishers, 2005). 110.

21. Malcolm Gladwell, *The Tipping Point* (New York: Little, Brown & Co., 2000), 7, 166.

22. Chip and Dan Heath, *Made to Stick* (New York: Random House: 2007), 240.

23. John D. Bransford, Ann L. Brown, and Rodney R. Cocking, eds. *How People Learn: Brain, Mind, Experience, and School*, Committee on Developments in the Science of Learning, National Research Council (Washington, DC: National Academy Press, 1999).

Chapter Four

Equip
(or, equip people with the understanding, motivation, and skills they need to see their new ideas through)

A detail from one of the nine collaborative power objects created through the Amherst Portraits Project. Each work, which is designed to reflect the local community, combines paint pen, oil pastel, spray enamel, and sign paint on billboard ink printing vinyl.

> The process of change is inherently constructivist. Any reform that is
> merely implemented will eventually recede rather than taking root. Each
> school community must struggle with new ideas for itself if it is to develop
> the deep understanding and commitment needed to engage in the continual
> problem-solving demanded by major changes in practice.
>
> —Linda Darling-Hammond

෴

In chapters 1–3, I outlined three foundational skills of leadership: self-awareness (Reflect), systems thinking (Connect), and shared decision making
(Create). Each skill is necessary and insufficient by itself, and, in an organizational context, each functions in a nonlinear fashion. It is only through the
combination of these abilities that leaders become more effective, and there
is no strict and surefire order one should follow in order to cultivate these
skills in himself and in others. As with everything else, human beings refuse
to behave so predictably.

There is, however, a general continuum of which we should be aware. At the
personal level, we begin by reflecting on "who's there." At the relational level,
we start to see how our behaviors contribute to the culture around us; gradually
we develop the capacity, with the help of others, to "see the whole board." At
the organizational level, we resist the urge to sell "our" ideas, opting instead to
consistently invite others to co-construct the world we share with them.

When these three skills start to take root in individuals and the organizational
culture of which they're a part, a palpable shift takes place. Transformational
change, and the collective will and clarity needed to achieve it, becomes possible. This doesn't mean transformational change will necessarily occur, only that
the proper conditions will have been created. At this point a fourth leadership
skill becomes necessary—ensuring that people have the understanding, motivation, and skills they need to continually work with the forces of change.

Working with the natural forces of change is very different from managing
change, just as cocreating a common vision is distinct from getting people to
"buy in." In one approach, schools and the individuals who inhabit them are
managed like machines, and people are given prepackaged "solutions" that
supersede community input; in the other, people and organizations are seen as
complex, living systems, and the inherent creativity and commitment of the
people being asked to change is what drives all decisions.

The fact that so many schools struggle to change core behaviors or processes is particularly troubling when one considers that, in essence, learning
itself is change. But the greater truth is that people don't resist change. They
resist being changed.

Knowing what will be easy and what will be difficult when it comes to whole-school renewal is essential for working with the natural forces of systemic change. And although there is no single way to be successful, there are different stages of the change process that can guide your community in its work together.

THE THREE STAGES OF CHANGE
—MIND, HEART, AND VOICE

We must experience an organizational change in three areas—our minds, our hearts, and our voices.

Here's what I mean by that: Before we are willing to change anything about our work or our behavior, we must first understand why the change is necessary and what it will require of us (mind). To actively participate in a major change initiative, we must feel intrinsically motivated in some way to contribute (heart). And to follow through on our individual and shared visions of an ideal learning community, we must have the skills and capabilities to not only demonstrate new behaviors but also ensure greater alignment between our internal passions and our external actions (voice).

Often, what happens in school improvement initiatives is we pay attention to some, but not all, of these stages. Teachers are asked to adopt a new teaching style before they fully understand why they should do so. Schools in search of more parent participation fail to explicitly consider what it will take to motivate greater numbers of adults to get involved. And students are invited to play a more active role in school governance before they've been equipped with the skills they need to do so effectively and responsibly.

Implicit in all of these scenarios is the recognition that implementing school-wide change requires an approach that encompasses individual, group, and organizational learning needs. Some of these needs will be simple, visible, and straightforward, such as providing basic information; others will be intangible, invisible, and elusive, such as addressing basic human emotions (see table 4.1).

Because organizational change always involves human perceptions and motivations, there are numerous lessons from the private sector that can help inform how to think about school improvement. In their book chronicling a major restructuring initiative at the consumer electronic retailer Best Buy, authors Elizabeth Gibson and Andy Billings underscore the universality of these distinctly human elements of change:

> Getting merchandise out on the shelves at the right time, staffing the service counter with the right number of people and within the labor budgets—these are the "hard" or concrete issues and they are the easiest to assess and change.

Table 4.1   What We Feel During Change

✓ A loss of control and stability	✓ A fear of letting go what worked in the past
✓ A high degree of uncertainty	✓ A high degree of stress
✓ A tendency to mistrust	✓ A high degree of energy, often undirected
✓ A reversion to a "me" focus	✓ A spike in conflicts of opinion and interest

By contrast, the "soft" issues are more difficult . . . *and* they are the heart of transformational change. The tangible features may represent the face of change, but the human factors—dealing with uncertainty, motivating and energizing people, and creating behavioral change—are critical to success. When soft issues are not addressed, the organization and its people appear resistant to change. As with any large system, organizations have their own inertia. Resistance, though an inevitable feature of change, becomes the convenient term for failure to address the soft side of change.[1]

Understanding the forces of change in this way places a unique set of challenges on a school leader, who must balance the community's attention to both hard (visible) and soft (invisible) issues. Other insights from the private sector underscore this point and help clarify the optimal role for principals to play in schoolwide improvement. Harvard Business School professors Michael Beer, Russell Eisenstat, and Bert Spector explain: "The most effective managers [in a multiyear study] recognized their limited power to mandate corporate renewal from the top. Instead, they defined their roles as creating a climate for change, then spreading the lessons of both successes and failures."[2] Management consultant Jim Collins puts it another way: "True leadership only exists if people follow when they have the freedom not to."[3]

Because organizational change is such a nonlinear experience, and because it requires leaders to both engender a sense of order (as opposed to control) and give people the freedom to coauthor the process, it's easy to feel overwhelmed about what to do. I believe the three-stage framework of mind, heart, and voice can help for two reasons: First, it provides a guide for school leaders that helps explain human, group, and organizational behavior in any major change initiative. Second, it can also be used as a framework for outlining a specific set of knowledge, skills, and dispositions schools should strive to cultivate throughout its student, faculty, and parent communities.

ROGER WILLIAMS MIDDLE SCHOOL
—A HYPOTHETICAL CASE STUDY

In part II, you'll read three case studies of real schools that have worked with the forces of change over several years to try and create stronger school cultures. Here, I want to provide a hypothetical example that can outline the dual utility of the change process I've just described.

To do so let's imagine a school (we'll call it Roger Williams Middle School) that has, over the past five years, actively worked to strengthen its organizational culture to positively impact student achievement and engagement. The school has anchored its work in the active cultivation of three sets of "civic habits"—of mind, heart, and voice—throughout the community.

It's important to note that these habits should not be construed as a readily exportable common vocabulary for schools across the country. They are meant instead to illuminate the major phases of change and spark your thinking about what a major change initiative might look like at the local level. As with everything else, what will be most valuable to your own community are the ideas and dreams that already exist there, not someone else's predetermined path (it's the process, not "the list"). So, please take from this section everything that is meaningful, discard everything that is not, and modify whatever will be helpful to drive your community's local work.

Year 1

The civic habits of mind, heart, and voice at Roger Williams Middle School were first identified five years ago. After gathering baseline data describing student, teacher, and parent attitudes and perceptions about school culture, community involvement, and student achievement, the school principal invited the community to have a series of conversations about what its students should be able to know about themselves, their academic subjects, and the world. Everyone in the community, old and young, was invited to these initial meetings, which were all framed by the simple question, "What does the ideal graduate of Roger Williams Middle School know how to do?"

The meetings were held at several different times, and in several different locations, to guarantee the broadest number of participants. Some meetings were highly structured, using either group-visioning exercises or specific dialogue protocols. Others were kept more informal. Detailed minutes of each meeting were kept and shared openly with anyone that wanted to see what had been discussed.

Gradually the community identified a set of academic habits that were specific to each department. These were to be used in helping each discipline reconsider its curricula and ensure that class time was being constructively used toward equipping young people with the skills and understanding they needed to be successful. But something else emerged—a set of core civic dispositions for not just a Roger Williams graduate, but also any responsible citizen.

These civic standards, equally important to the academic standards, allowed the community to spend time envisioning what each behavior would actually look like when a person had achieved personal mastery. This list was published in draft form and distributed throughout the community (a partial sample is provided in table 4.2).

By the time June rolled around, Roger Williams had decided to hold a celebratory picnic to honor its work. Over the course of a school year, the community had identified what it valued most, and it had begun creating a common vocabulary to describe it. Now the challenge was to flesh out each

Table 4.2 Roger Williams Middle School—Civic Habits of Mind, Heart, and Voice

	Mind	Heart	Voice
Key Issue to Overcome	Lack of Understanding	Lack of Motivation	Lack of Skills
Key Objective	All people involved with the school understand why student voice matters, and why their participation is essential to strengthening school culture	All people involved with the school are motivated to use their voices to help create a safer, more equitable climate that can support student learning	All people involved with the school feel they have voice, value, and visibility, and every person has the skills they need to be seen and heard in constructive ways
Desired Civic Habit (What the end result will *look like*)	Value inquiry that encourages and appreciates both complexity and ambiguity	Take responsibility for self and others, and resolve differences in constructive ways	Listen and observe deeply, and respond in a way that helps to connect to others
Desired Civic Habit	Demonstrate knowledge of democratic principles, human rights, and social justice	Demonstrate clarity of moral purpose	Exercise free speech responsibility, and always speak out on matters of conscience
Desired Civic Habit	Practice critical reflection of self and others	Act with courage and compassion	Agree and disagree honestly and respectfully
Desired Civic Habit	Understand how to participate in the political processes and institutions that shape public policy	Practice forgiveness and humility	Believe that how we debate, not just what we debate, is critical

habit more fully, so people could track the evolution of their own understanding over time.

Year 2

The following August, the principal convened a smaller focus group of faculty and parent volunteers, and asked them to create a draft set of behavioral rubrics for each habit. These rubrics, he carefully explained, would eventually be used to assess individual understanding, help the school determine if it was making progress toward its goals, and ensure that everyone—from the administrators to the students—was clear about what the school valued and what it wanted its future graduates to learn and value.

After many meetings and conversations, the group announced that its rubrics were ready to be shared. Teachers took the rubrics into their advisory classes and asked their students to provide feedback and revisions. Eventually, thanks to a student recommendation, the rubrics were extended to include a fifth cell. A sample looked like the one in table 4.3.

The process of cocreating the habits—and the clarity they provided to students, teachers, and parents—helped create a different atmosphere at the school. It was still too early to see statistical improvements in student achievement, and yet as year 2 drew to a close, the principal could already point to more positive student, faculty, and parent attitudes about the school,

Table 4.3   An Evaluative Rubric from Roger Williams Middle School

Beginner	Novice	Advanced	Competent	Proficient	Expert
Respect and Advocacy (Desired Civic Habit)	Does not speak up to offer own opinions; does not care about ideas shared by others	Occasionally exercises free speech to offer own opinions; listens to some of what others say	Speaks about own opinions with honesty; asks for feedback; listens respectfully	Exercises free speech responsibly and honestly; asks for feedback; listens respectfully	Exercises free speech responsibly, honestly, and with clarity; always speaks out on matters of conscience; asks for and responds to feedback; balances advocacy with inquiry

thanks to the biannual use of attitudinal surveys of all stakeholders. Student attendance had improved, and the number of student referrals for misbehavior had declined.

Year 3

By the start of year 3, it felt as though people were starting to think less about their individual experiences at the school ("What's in it for me?") and more about working together for the common good ("What's in it for us?"). A greater awareness and appreciation of democratic principles was also evident among parents, teachers, and students. In short, people were starting to think about their individual rights and their civic responsibilities to each other. They were starting to connect the use of those freedoms to the quality of their community. And they were able to articulate what the desired behaviors and skills were supposed to look like—both in themselves and in others (see table 4.4).

Still, challenges remained. Despite the principal's best intentions, certain people seemed stubbornly intent on sidestepping the process. It had also become clear that certain teaching styles were better suited to the desired outcomes than others. And a few people had started to get identified as the movers and shakers of the school, leaving others feeling left out, jealous, or invisible.

Table 4.4   Roger Williams Middle School: Year Three Outcomes

Self-assessment reports (mid-year and year-end)

A greater integration between assessment and instruction, such that a variety of methods are used and assessment is not just a measure of student achievement but also a part of the learning process itself

A written and aligned curriculum for each content area that is, where practical, connected to real-life applications of knowledge and skills and the adoption of specific measurements for the civic habits of mind, heart, and voice

A staff development calendar that reflects staff needs and desires and a school schedule that provides teachers with structured opportunities to reflect on and improve each other's practices

On- and off-site training in democratic processes for school stakeholders

The creation of new programs and structures that engage and empower youth voice, such as youth governance, youth media, and service learning

Initial quantitative and qualitative evidence that stakeholder perceptions, school safety, teacher satisfaction and student achievement have improved

In response, the principal resolved neither to become consumed by the 5 percent of the faculty that was uninvolved, nor to forget about and ignore them. He continued inviting (and inviting again) new voices to join the leadership team and subcommittees that were supporting the school's holistic reform plans. He ensured, thanks to the help of the district office, that the school's professional development calendar was aligned to equip teachers with the skills they would need to be successful. And he explored new ways for adults and young people to actively participate in the life of the school. As year 3 drew to a close, he wondered if the progress the school had made this far could be sustained.

Year 4

As year 4 reached the halfway point, student achievement and behavior continued to improve, and the school started to receive national attention for its work. Despite the positive attention, a number of new teachers, students, and families had not been part of the initial discussions about the school's academic and civic habits; the community had changed. The principal perceived that the habits were less alive at the school than they had been before. Perhaps the newer community members felt the whole process was mechanistic. Perhaps the veterans who helped launch the process now felt a sense of disrespect from these new colleagues for what they had worked so hard to create.

The principal wondered if he was witnessing an implementation dip. The shared enthusiasm for the work had ebbed, new faces had entered, and the community had been reconstituted. What had worked so well in the past was in need of some revisiting.

At first the principal planned to ask the faculty what was wrong with the habits and if they felt like revisiting them. Then he decided to adopt a more open-ended approach. To help the faculty examine and assess its own commitment to the school's emphasis on the civic habits, the principal gave them a chance to reflect together on the good, the bad, and the ugly at the school. At a faculty meeting, he used a NSRF protocol, Microlabs (see figure 4.1), to let the faculty reflect in triads on three questions:

1. What would a visitor to our school describe as its most visible characteristics?
2. What would a veteran of our school describe as its most invisible characteristics?
3. Based on your answers to the first two questions, what implications do you see for our work going forward?

National
School
Reform
Faculty

Harmony
Education   www.nsrfharmony.org
Center

Microlabs

*These guidelines and questions were adapted from those developed by Julian Weissglass for the National
Coalition for Equity in Education based at the University of California, Santa Barbara.*

Purpose
To address a specific sequence of questions in a structured format with small groups, using active listening
skills.

Time allotted
About 8 minutes per question — this works best with a series of no more than three questions.

Group format
Form triads — either with the people you're sitting near — or find others in the group you don't know
well. Number off — 1, 2, 3.

Facilitation Tips
"I'll direct what we will talk about. Each person will have one minute (or, sometimes, 2 minutes,
depending on the group and the question) to talk about a question when it's their turn. While the person is
speaking, the other two in the group simply listen. When the time is up, the next person speaks, and so on.
I'll tell you when to switch." Emphasize that talk has to stop when you call time, and conversely, that if the
person is done speaking before time is up, the three people should sit in silence, using the time to reflect.
Review the Guidelines (previous page).

The quality of the questions matter in this exercise. The questions should be ones that are important to the
group.

The Activity
After instructing the group, read the first question aloud (twice). Give everyone time to write in
preparation. Then, tell people when to begin, and then tell them when each one/two minute segment is up.
On the first question, begin with person #1, then #2, then #3. Then read the next question aloud. On the
second question, begin with #2, then #3, then #1. On the third question, begin with #3, then #1, then #2.

Reflection questions following the activity
• What did you hear that was significant? What key ideas or insights were shared?
• How did this go for you? What worked well, and what was difficult? Why?
• How might your conversations have been different had we not used this protocol?
• What are the advantages/disadvantages of using this activity? When would you use this protocol?
• What would you want to keep in mind as someone facilitating this activity?

Protocols are most powerful and effective when used within an ongoing professional learning community such as a Critical Friends Group® and facilitated
by a skilled coach. To learn more about professional learning communities and seminars for new or experienced coaches, please visit the National School
Reform Faculty website at www.nsrfharmony.org.

Figure 4.1.   The Microlabs protocol.

After each person answered the questions privately, the principal broke
the teachers into unusual small-group configurations. Teachers who didn't
always work together had the first opportunity to discuss their answers
with each other. A second round of conversations then took place with
the teachers back in their usual grade- or subject-specific teams. Finally,

the principal facilitated a large-group conversation in which people were encouraged to speak freely. Because the school had established such clear expectations for respectful debate and behavior, group norms were easy to follow.

What emerged from the conversation was not what the principal expected. There was no larger cultural crisis, it turned out, nor had the habits lost their meaning. In fact, the principal learned, the teachers had implemented their own unofficial orientation for new teachers that oriented them to the culture of the school.

What had changed was the number of opportunities faculty members had to communicate with each other. The principal realized that once common planning time for teachers was added to the schedule, he'd incorrectly assumed they had everything they needed. He'd stopped using CFG dialogue protocols at faculty meetings, and he'd become less explicit about making sure the teachers had opportunities to clarify what was working and what wasn't in their professional practices (see Table 4.5). The principal resolved to give the community what it was asking for—more structured opportunities to connect with, support, and learn from each other.

Year 5

As Roger Williams Middle School was preparing to graduate its latest class of eighth graders, the principal paused to reflect on how far the community had come. Its campus had become a more effective, efficient, and equitable place. There was demonstrable evidence—thanks to disciplinary report data and school safety surveys—that students felt safer and more empowered than they did five years ago. The school's cocreated civic habits of mind, heart, and voice were now an established part of the student evaluation system, and students and teachers were encouraged to self-evaluate themselves on a regular basis. Best of all student learning had improved. The faculty played a much more active role in determining its own professional development needs, and the schedule had been adjusted to ensure more common planning time for teachers. When disagreements arose between espoused beliefs and the school's actual practices, grievances were negotiated openly and respectfully. New structures had emerged to support the collective vision of the community as well, providing increased opportunities for adults and young people to use their voices and share responsibility for shaping school culture (see Table 4.6).

In five years, Roger Williams Middle School had started to become the type of school its community envisioned. And the work had just begun.

Table 4.5   Working with the Three Stages of Change

Stages	Habits of Mind (Understanding)	Habits of Heart (Motivation)	Habits of Voice (Skills)
Key Questions	• What is the core issue we are trying to address with these changes? • What does a strong school culture look like? • What does any of this have to do with teaching and learning? • What will this require of me? • How will we know if we've been successful? • Why is my involvement necessary?	• Why do we think implementing these ideas will cause the change that's needed? • What's our theory of change? • What's in it for me? • For what am I accountable? • What are the consequences for not changing? • Am I capable of this? • Do I want to be a part of this?	• What will I need to start doing differently? • What new processes must I follow? • How will I learn to do this? • Will I get to practice these skills, and will I receive any feedback? • Who already does this well, and how can I learn from then?
Key Actions	• Seek understanding • Take the pulse of the school • Start with a strong *intention* - not action plans • Create the conditions that allow people to clarify their personal visions and tell their stories • Begin with changes that are easy, significant, and achievable • Tolerate messiness • Don't try to tell people what to think	• Strengthen the web of relationships by building a shared sense of purpose • Be comfortable with the 'discomfort' of people's fears and ideas • Help people imagine what it will feel like when it works • Celebrate the early successes • Don't just acknowledge the people who "play by the rules"; honor the respectful dissenters	• Create detailed rubrics of the new behaviors • Provide intensive feedback, and chart your progress • Reward, coach, and reinforce new, emerging behaviors • Align incentives to reinforce the new behaviors • Unlearn the incompatible behaviors

Table 4.6 Cultivating the Civic Habits of Mind, Heart and Voice Through the Change Process

Reflect (Seeing the need)	Connect (Cultivating the skills)	Create (Sustaining the vision)
• Create space for people to reflect on what is meaningful to them as human beings • Inquire together about the meaning of work and the needs of young people • Discuss the connection between healthy schools and the responsible use of democratic skills • Learn to identify the organization's explicit and implicit goals • Look for patterns, not data points • Determine how the old culture influences behavior through recognitions, rewards, etc. • Confront old behaviors and ways of seeing • Decide together what is meaningful and what behaviors need to change • Map archetypal behaviors of the old and the desired behaviors of the new culture	• Identify what's working, what isn't, and what people want to change • Explore individual and group fears • Identify the words and language that can articulate the new vision • Create rubrics that clarify what new behaviors should look like • Ensure that professional development training is aligned with the skills people will need to see through the desired changes • Eliminate organizational roadblocks to learning • Provide opportunities for people to talk about the new shared purpose and the meaning of change • Provide opportunities for people to practice and reinforce the new behaviors • Encourage the direct discussion of losses and concerns • Celebrate early successes	• Use appropriate assessment measures to track changes over time • Create open channels for feedback and questioning • Invite, and then invite again, anyone who has not felt included in the process • Compare "then" and "now" to track how far the organization has come • Continually explore gaps between the present reality and the shared goals • Realign rewards and recognition to support new values, beliefs and behaviors • Keep asking, "What behaviors are we rewarding?" • Follow the meaning; resist a blind adherence to "the plan" • Raise expectations • Provide balanced feedback • Give people ongoing opportunities to exercise their voices and revisit the vision if necessary • Emphasize and share all assessment data

⌒✐⌒

Although the specific story of Roger Williams Middle School is fictional, all of its insights and challenges come from real schools that achieved real improvement in student learning using a similar approach to whole-school improvement. And although the school's principal plays an essential role in the process, it's important to note how he recognizes he does not need to be—indeed, should not be—the person most identified with the good work of the school.

Because he understands the nature of organizational change processes, the principal understands that his task is to make the process of change meaningful to people from the start, to create conditions that allow for their full participation, and to provide an environment in which creativity can flourish. He does not need to have all the answers ahead of time, or expend energy trying to get everyone on board. His job is simply to keep everyone feeling connected to each other and the school's shared vision—and, if need be, to create the space for the community to revisit its goals. And his course of action, determined by his understanding of the change process itself, is to ensure that all people have the understanding (mind), the motivation (heart), and the skills (voice) they need to create the type of culture the group has envisioned together.

All of these actions still don't guarantee that major change will take place. They do, however, greatly increase the likelihood that people will participate in the co-creation of a healthier, higher-functioning organizational culture.

Take the time to know who's there. Make the connections that help you see the whole board. Remember that people only support what they create. And ensure that all stakeholders are equipped with the understanding, motivation, and skills they need to work with the forces of change.

Reflect. Connect. Create. Equip.

There's one foundational skill left. And it's perhaps the most important—and difficult—to cultivate.

EQUIP—FIVE THINGS YOU CAN DO

Read *The Right to Learn*

As the United States transitions into a new century—and a more interconnected, interdependent world—our schools must also make a transition. Never before has the success (perhaps even the survival) of nations and people been so tightly tied to their ability to learn. "Consequently," writes

Stanford University professor Linda Darling-Hammond, "our future depends now, as never before, on our ability to teach."

"Over the last decade," Darling-Hammond explains, "reformers have created and redesigned thousands of schools that are now educating rich and poor, black, brown, and white students alike to levels of success traditionally thought impossible to achieve. Yet these schools remain at the margins, rarely embraced or supported by the systems in which they struggle to exist and generally unexamined for what they can teach the education enterprise. This book asks how we can reinvent the system of U.S. public education so that it ensures a right to learn for all of its students, who will enter a world in which a failure to learn is fast becoming an insurmountable defeat."

Take a Learning Style Self-Assessment

Bernice McCarthy's 4MAT system, a synthesis of numerous researchers' work, identifies four archetypal learning styles: imaginative, analytic, common sense, and dynamic. The characteristics of each are derived largely from the intersection of two continua. The first is how we perceive information, and where we fall along the continuum of experiencing-feeling-thinking. The second is how we process the information we have taken in and the pace at which we move from reflective to active processing.

Understanding how we learn has major implications for our understanding of how we see (and fail to see) the world around us.

To identify your personal learning style, visit www.aboutlearning.com.

Host a World Café Conversation

As a conversational process, the World Café is an innovative yet simple methodology for hosting conversations about questions that matter. These conversations link and build on each other as people move between groups, cross-pollinate ideas, and discover new insights into the questions or issues that are most important in their life, work, or community. As a process, the World Café can evoke and make visible the collective intelligence of any group, thus increasing people's capacity for effective action in pursuit of common aims.

For more information, visit www.theworldcafe.com.

Make Clarity (of Purpose and Roles) Your Constant Goal

Often, the best-intentioned school change initiatives get derailed by some combination of the following shortcomings:

- a lack of clarity over what needs to be changed;
- a lack of understanding about the skills people will need in order to see the changes through;
- a lack of consideration for the pace at which the changes should occur.

To guard against these pitfalls, it may be helpful to use the following questions:

- *What*—What is it specifically you want to change?
- *Why*—Why does it matter?
- *How*—How will the proposed process get you there?
- *Who*—Who will be responsible for the different roles and responsibilities going forward? Who has been a part of the decision-making process thus far? Who else needs to know about what is being planned?
- *When*—When (and how) will you know you've been successful?

Trust the Process (and Track Your Progress)

If you've been attentive to the natural evolution of the change process, your community will be sure to take several steps to prepare itself for a successful change initiative. Use the tables from this chapter to ensure that you've taken appropriate steps along the way.

NOTES

1. Elizabeth Gibson and Andy Billings, *Big Change at Best Buy* (Palo Alto, CA: Davies-Black Publishing, 2003), 52.
2. Michael Beer, Russell A. Eisenstat, and Bert Spector, "Why Change Programs Don't Produce Change," *Harvard Business Review* (November–December 1990): 5.
3. Jim Collins, *Good to Great in the Social Sector* (Boulder: Jim Collins, 2005), 13.

Chapter Five

Let Come
(or, practice "urgent patience"
to let the school's shared vision
come naturally into being)

One of the six public installations composed of eighteen large-scale public works made by students, faculty, and staff from Amherst College, all of which focus on community reflections of the educational community.

Do your work, then step back. The only path to serenity.

—Lao Tzu

∽⦿∾

In the world of Edward Lorenz's computer, the sun never stopped shining, day never gave way to night, and clouds could not exist.

It was 1960, so the bulky machine, distended with wires and vacuum tubes, lacked the speed and capacity to realistically simulate the earth's atmosphere. Yet Lorenz's computer quickly became the talk of his MIT colleagues. All day, it printed out row upon row of numbers based on twelve numerical rules—equations that expressed the relationship between temperature, air pressure, wind speed, and so forth. From the printouts, Lorenz and his colleagues made educated guesses about what the weather would do next. Sometimes they guessed right, yet nothing happened the same way twice. Ever.

This last fact challenged the Newtonian worldview scientists had learned to revere. Understand the laws of physics, generations had been told, and you can understand the workings of the universe. As one scientist explained, "You're taught that there are classical models where everything is determined by initial conditions, and then there are quantum mechanical models where things are determined but you have to contend with a limit on how much initial information you can gather. *Nonlinear* was a word you only encountered in the back of the book."[1]

Lorenz had two resources Newton couldn't have imagined—the digital computer and the space satellite—that promised to accelerate mankind's eventual mastery of the natural world and all its secrets. For a time, Lorenz even believed he had programmed his computer to reduce the behavior of the weather into some generally recognizable patterns. He was sounding a lot like the eighteenth-century mathematician Pierre-Simon Laplace, who saw amid the promise of Newtonian physics a world that "would embrace in the same formula the movements of the greatest bodies of the universe and those of the lightest atom; for it, nothing would be uncertain and the future, as the past, would be present to its eyes."[2]

There was, however, a small factor complicating this vision—measuring a system as complex as the weather can never be precise. Certitude is a chimera. As one theoretician often told his students: "The basic idea of Western science is that you don't have to take into account the falling of a leaf on some planet in another galaxy when you're trying to account for the motion of a billiard ball on a pool table on earth. Very small influences can be neglected. There's a convergence in the way things work, and arbitrarily small influences don't blow up to have arbitrarily large effects."[3]

One afternoon in 1961, Edward Lorenz unintentionally refuted this foundational idea of Western science. Instead of running the same group of numbers through the system from the start, Lorenz restarted the process halfway through and then left to get a cup of coffee. The new run should have mirrored the old, yet when he returned an hour later, Lorenz discovered a weather pattern that had completely diverged from its previous course.

Eventually he identified the difference in the two experiments: in the computer's memory, six decimal places were stored. On the printout, Lorenz had only entered the first three, assuming the one-part-in-a-thousand difference was inconsequential. It wasn't.

The implication was clear: even the tiniest variations warranted close scrutiny. The promise of long-range weather forecasting was illusory. And the butterfly effect—or the notion that a butterfly's wings in Beijing today could shape next month's weather pattern in New York City—was more than just idle chatter. As inconvenient as it may be to the scientific community, it was becoming clear that everything mattered. Lorenz explains:

> I think one of the reasons people thought it would be possible to forecast so far ahead," Lorenz explained, "is that there are real physical phenomena for which one can do an excellent job of forecasting, such as eclipses, where the dynamics of the sun, moon, and earth are fairly complicated, and such as oceanic tides. I never used to think of tide forecasts as prediction at all—I used to think of them as statements of fact—but of course, you are predicting. Tides are actually just as complicated as the atmosphere. Both have periodic components—you can predict that next summer will be warmer than this winter. But with weather we take the attitude that we knew *that* already. With tides, it's the predictable part that we're interested in, and the unpredictable part is small, unless there's a storm. But I realized that any physical system that behaved nonperiodically would be unpredictable.[4]

What Lorenz discovered, however, was more than the randomness of weather patterns; it was order masquerading as randomness. As James Gleick explains in *Chaos: Making a New Science*, Lorenz's accidental discovery helped launch a new scientific field, chaos theory:

> The simplest systems are now seen to create extraordinarily difficult problems of predictability. Yet order arises spontaneously in those systems—chaos and order together. Traditionally, when physicists saw complex results, they looked for complex causes. . . . The modern theory of chaos began with the creeping realization in the 1960s that . . . tiny differences in input could quickly become overwhelming differences in output—a phenomenon given the name "sensitive dependence on initial conditions.[5]

Since Lorenz's discovery, continued advancements in computer science—coupled with the irrepressible, ongoing desire to predict the future—have spurred further investment in all types of forecasting models, from the weather to the economy. Despite these advances, today's best weather machines remain purely speculative beyond two or three days and worthless as little as a week in advance.

Why do weather-forecasting systems continue to be so inaccurate? What is the relationship between chaos and order? And what does any of this have to do with human behavior and organizational leadership?

FREEDOM AND STRUCTURE: THE DELICATE BALANCE

"If we could change a society like we can change the position of the furniture in a house, it would be fantastic," said educator Paulo Freire in a 1987 address. "It would just be a question of muscular power. But history is not like this."[6]

Freire believed educators were particularly burdened by the challenges of change, because so many are "much more traditional and fear the students' possibilities more than they should. They could believe much more in the abilities of the students, of the people, but they are . . . conditioned by a very old fear, which is the fear of freedom."[7]

What unnerves us most about freedom is the same thing generations of scientists were unconsciously ignoring about the universe—its unpredictability and capacity for disorder. In the classroom, this fear of the unknown has misled many of us into thinking that the relationship between freedom and structure is an either/or proposition. As educators, we're either providing good, structured instruction, or we're refereeing spitball fights. But there's a difference between being authoritative and being authoritarian, a point Freire clarifies:

> The teacher has to teach, to experience, to *demonstrate* authority and the student has to experience freedom in relation to the teacher's authority. The authority of the teacher is absolutely necessary for the development of the freedom of the students, but if the authority of the teacher goes beyond the limits authority has to have in relation to the students' freedom, then we no longer have authority. We no longer have freedom. We have *authoritarianism.*[8]

Freire recognized the creative tension that exists between individual freedom and group structure. Stanford professor Linda Darling-Hammond has written about it as well. "The middle ground between permissiveness and authoritarianism," she says, "is *authoritative practice.* Authoritative treatment sets limits and consequences within a context that fosters dialogue, explicit teaching about how to assume responsibility, and democratic decision-making."[9]

This distinction between authoritative and authoritarian practice is particularly resonant in the teacher-student dynamic (although it's central to all relationships, both personal and professional). Its implications are clear: the solution is not to choose between freedom and structure, but to strike the right balance between the two.

In the introduction I quoted Fred Givens, a principal at Bronx Prep Charter School in New York City, who explained what this delicate balance feels like. "Some of us," he says, "have learned that—despite what intuition might suggest—structure actually creates freedom. . . . It has become clear that the potential for looseness, play, free thought and creativity is generated when the structures are so tight and elegantly constructed that they become nearly invisible. This has been a fundamental revelation."[10]

As scientists like Lorenz have observed, the Newtonian dream of certainty cannot be comprehensively quantified. And as educators like Givens have witnessed, a healthy sense of group order (as opposed to control) cannot be imposed from the top down or the outside in. Instead, as chaos theory instructs, order emerges as elements of a given system—from a school to the universe—interact and settle into patterns. And even then, the patterns are always changing.

In scientific terms, this is because every piece (or person) of a dynamic system that can move independently introduces another variable, or degree of freedom, to the equation. Chaos—or unpredictability—is actually a stable, structured element of any such system. Even more remarkable, it's precisely that unpredictable behavior that, in time, can help produce order, spur creativity, and allow the rhythms of life to survive and evolve. "Here was one coin with two sides," explained the scientist Doyne Farmer, talking about chaos theory. "Here was order, with randomness emerging, and then one step further away was randomness with its own underlying order."[11]

Apply this thinking to a school environment and you're likely to develop very different theories about the best way to establish order (as opposed to control) and support student learning. As Meg Wheatley argues, a paradoxical truism emerges: the more freedom the organization has to organize itself, the more order it enjoys.

> This is, for me, the most illuminating paradox of all. The two forces that we have placed in opposition to one another—freedom and order—turn out to be partners in generating healthy, well-ordered systems. Effective self-organization is supported by two critical elements: a clear sense of identity, and freedom. In organizations, if people are free to make their own decisions, guided by a clear organizational identity for them to reference, the whole system develops greater coherence and strength. The organization is less controlling, but more orderly.[12]

LETTING NEW IDEAS COME NATURALLY INTO BEING

One of the great paradoxes of human beings is that we feel two pressing needs at the same time—the freedom that comes from defining ourselves as individuals, and the security that comes from feeling connected to one another. Sometimes, this paradox leads us to satisfy one need at the expense of the other. But these two impulses are not mutually exclusive. To join an orderly community, we are not required to abandon the freedom to express our individuality. And to be free, we do not need to sacrifice our sense of security, our commitment to order, or the meaningful connections we make in our relationships with others.

A similar paradox is at play in our society at large and in our organizations. What is a school principal—or any organizational leader, for that matter—supposed to do with this information?

If you've come this far, I hope you have a sense by now of where (and how) to start: take the time to know who's there; make the connections that let you see the whole board; empower people to cocreate the environment they share; and equip everyone with what they need to see their ideas through.

When an organization's fertile topsoil has been carefully cultivated in this way, the fifth foundation of leadership—letting come—becomes essential. We know, for example, that transformational leaders help people develop clarity about themselves and the inner place from which they operate, and that they create conditions that support people's efforts to fulfill their potential. Sometimes we make the mistake of thinking that to create such a climate, the leader must essentially let go of the reins. But there's a difference between letting go of one's responsibility, which is an abdication of leadership, and letting go of old mental models and habits, which we must do to create the space that will allow new ways of seeing and thinking to come into being.

The biologist, philosopher, and cognitive scientist Francisco Varela dedicated his career to exploring how this evolution works. Varela's work helped MIT professor Otto Scharmer map the letting-go process in three stages:

> First, you help the group *suspend* judgments in order to see the objective reality they are up against. Second, you help them *redirect* their attention from the object to the process in order to help them view the system from a perspective that allows them to see how their own actions contribute to the problem at hand. It is at that point that people begin to see themselves as part of the issue, they begin to see how they collectively create a pattern that at first seemed to be caused by purely exterior forces. And then, if you're lucky, you can bring them to a *deeper place of stillness* where they let go of the old and start to connect with their higher-order intentions.[13]

The challenge of modern leadership, then, involves knowing which old habits and ideas we must let go of so that new habits and ideas can emerge. That process will always involve some uncertainty and discomfort. Indeed, allowing yourself to be uncertain of what will emerge is the threshold we must pass through for new ways of being to take root. As Scharmer explains,

> Letting go and surrendering can be thought of as two sides of the same coin. Letting go concerns the opening process, the removal of barriers and junk in one's way, and surrendering is moving into the resulting opening. . . . [When this happens] we see the same fundamental happening: the arrival, the beginning birth, and the coming into being of a new self, the essential or authentic self that connects us with who we really are.[14]

Clearly, old ways of thinking and managing that no longer serve us are things we should let go of. And yet developing the capacity to let those ideas go is precisely what allows for the possibility of something new to emerge. If we as leaders are committed less to hierarchical organizations and a better balance between freedom and structure, we must trust the processes we put in place (see chapters 1–4) and resist the traditional tendency to have a vividly preconceived notion of what the end result will look like. It's about a shared vision, after all. As Robert Greenleaf observes in his classic treatise, *The Servant as Leader*, "The freer the institution and the more scope for autonomy and initiative given to individuals . . . the more important is the role of the many informal leaders among all constituencies: students, faculty, administration."[15]

If a principal has consciously cultivated the first four foundational skills of leadership at her school, it's highly likely that many small movements have already begun to take root. (A sort of order, perhaps, masquerading as chaos?) From here, three simple principles can guide the work moving forward and help the principal practice the urgent patience necessary to let a free and responsible school culture come naturally into being.

Less Structure

Finding the balance between too much and too little structure is a key to developing the organizational capacity to change and thrive. Too often schools and organizations lead with more structures—from working groups to grading policies—and then expect the necessary knowledge, commitment, and results to follow.

Try this instead: Before rushing to create any new structures (or working groups, or committees, etc.), find out first if there's a need for them. Help your community concentrate its initial energies on identifying its greatest needs. The structures you need to address the problems they identify will evolve naturally. As Wheatley says, "We need leaders to understand that we are best controlled by concepts that invite our participation, not policies and procedures that curtail our contribution."[16]

More Information

In Tom Friedman's book *The World is Flat*, Yahoo! cofounder Jerry Yang talks about how the "democratization of information" has impacted societies across the globe.

> Today's consumers are much more efficient—they can find information, products, services, faster [through search engines] than through traditional means. They are better informed about issues related to work, health, leisure, etc. Small towns are no longer disadvantaged relative to those with better access to information. And people have the ability to be better connected to things that interest them, to quickly and easily become experts in given subjects and to connect with others who share their interests.[17]

Although Yang is talking about the global marketplace, the same ideas hold true for organizations. How freely does information travel in your organization? Is there a sense of knowledge equity, such that any two people in the school at any time are likely to have the same access to information? Or are some people more privy to key knowledge than others? How rapidly does bad news travel upward?

Knowing the answers to these questions tells us a lot about an organization (or a society), its commitment to freedom, and how well—or poorly—it has created a climate of trust and transparency.

More (Civil) Friction

In the scientific world, nonlinear systems (like the weather) defy simple explanation. That's why, historically, nonlinear terms have been omitted when people want to get a clear, simple understanding of things.

Take friction. As James Gleick explains,

> Without friction a simple linear equation expresses the amount of energy you need to accelerate a hockey puck. With friction the relationship gets complicated, because the amount of energy changes depending on how fast the puck is already moving. Nonlinearity means the act of playing the game has a way of changing the rules. You cannot assign a constant importance to friction, because its importance depends on speed. Speed, in turn, depends on friction. That twisted changeability makes nonlinearity hard to calculate, but it also creates rich kinds of behavior that never occur in linear systems.[18]

The same is true of democracies and school cultures. When we allow all voices to be heard, and when we engender a respectful exchange of ideas, we invite the creative power of civil friction. "One of the most reliable indicators of a team that is continually learning is the visible conflict of ideas," Peter Senge explains. "In great teams conflict becomes productive. There may, and often will, be conflict around the vision. In fact, the essence of the 'visioning' process lies in the gradual emergence of a shared vision from different personal visions. . . . Conflict becomes, in effect, part of the ongoing dialogue."[19]

The importance of civil friction is also the core idea behind the First Amendment. Charles Haynes, the First Amendment Center's senior scholar and a national authority on religious liberty issues, believes a deeper understanding of the First Amendment's five freedoms (religion, speech, press, assembly, petition) can even help schools find common ground on the issues that most deeply divide them. "We have found," he says, "that where communities are committed to coming together in the spirit of the First Amendment, consensus is reached, new policies are drafted, and significant changes take place in the classroom."[20]

At the heart of that spirit is a framework for civil friction that Haynes calls the "Three R's":

- **Rights:** The First Amendment's guarantee to protect freedom of conscience is a precious, fundamental and inalienable right for all. Every effort should be made in public schools to protect the consciences of all people.
- **Responsibilities:** Central to the notion of the common good is the recognition that the First Amendment's five freedoms (religion, speech, press, assembly, petition) are universal rights joined to a universal duty to respect the rights of others. Rights are best guarded and responsibilities best exercised when each person and group guards for all others those rights they wish guarded for themselves.
- **Respect:** Conflict and debate are vital to democracy. Yet if controversies about freedom in schools are to reflect the highest wisdom of the First Amendment and advance the best interest of the nation, *how* we debate, and not only *what* we debate, is critical.[21]

Paolo Freire agrees. "The more people participate in the process of their own education, the more the people participate in the process of defining what kind of production to produce, and for what and why, the more the people participate in the development of their selves. The more the people become themselves, the better the democracy."[22]

When I was a boy, my hometown in New Hampshire experienced a massive snowstorm. Like all children, I spent every possible minute outside, watching the thousands of different snowflakes fall to the ground, or, if I was lucky, land on the tip of my tongue.

I didn't care then that each one was different. But as an adult I wondered what could account for such complexity in such small things. Then I read James Gleick's *Chaos*, and I understood.

> Sensitive dependence on initial conditions serves not to destroy but to create. As a growing snowflake falls to earth, typically floating in the wind for an hour or more, the choices made by the branching tips at any instant depend sensitively on such things as the temperature, the humidity, and the presence of impurities in the atmosphere. The six tips of a single snowflake, spreading within a millimeter space, feel the same temperatures, and because the laws of growth are purely deterministic, they maintain a near-perfect symmetry. But the nature of turbulent air is such that any pair of snowflakes will experience very different paths. *The final flake records the history of all the changing weather conditions it has experienced, and the combinations may as well be infinite.* (italics added)[23]

What a perfect parallel to the challenges our nation's schools—and young people—face every day. Sensitive dependence on initial conditions. A system that must serve to create. And a "final flake" that will reflect the history of everything it has experienced.

LET COME—FIVE THINGS YOU CAN DO

Read *The Long Haul*

The Long Haul is the autobiography of Myles Horton, whose Highlander Folk School helped train civil rights activists like Martin Luther King Jr., Rosa Parks, and Eleanor Roosevelt. In chronicling the evolution of Highlander, Horton traces his own thought process, providing a useful example of how one person struggled with an idea over time in order to allow a powerful organizational vision to come into being.

Experiment with Open Space Technology

In the book *Open Space Technology*, Harrison Owen provides a user's guide for those interested in using open space technology (OST)—an organic way of structuring group conversations that harnesses the level of synergy and excitement found during the coffee break conversations at more traditional meetings.

As Owen explains, "OST is effective in situations where a diverse group of people must deal with complex and potentially conflicting material in innovative and productive ways. It is particularly powerful when nobody knows the answer and the ongoing participation of a number of people is required to deal with the questions. Conversely, OST will not work, and therefore should not be used, in any situation where the answer is already known, where somebody at a high level *thinks* the answer is already known, or where somebody is the sort that *must* know the answer, and therefore must always be in charge, otherwise known as control, control, control."

Let Go of Old Habits and Ways of Seeing

To allow new ways of thinking to emerge, we must be willing to confront, and then let go of, the mental models that no longer serve us. For some of us, this may be a traditional approach to classroom management, a particular style of interpersonal communication, or a tendency to define the origins of problems as "out there" instead of "in here." Whatever the answers may be, the way we find them is by practicing self-reflection, intentionally and consistently, with courage, humility, and openness to the discovery of something new.

Don't Let Go of Everything

There is a key distinction between letting go of the mental models and habits that no longer serve you well—which is essential if new ideas and ways of being are to emerge—and letting go of the decision-making process entirely, which is an abdication of leadership.

Create the space that lets people develop greater clarity of themselves and the organization they are a part of. Do not stand back and wait for innovation to emerge. Self-organization does not just self-organize, after all; it needs someone to prepare the soil.

Practice Urgent Patience

Research confirms that before lasting change can take root, people must acquire the understanding, the motivation, and the skills they need to see their new ideas through. By definition, this type of transformation, at both the individual and organizational levels, takes time.

A central challenge for all of us, then, is to become what leadership consultant Cile Chavez calls a mystic—or, someone with a distant vision and an up-close focus. We must have clarity about where our work is headed and how we'll know when we get there. And we must have patience, so that new ideas and behaviors can get baked into the culture of the school.

NOTES

1. James Gleick, *Chaos: Making a New Science* (New York: Penguin Books, 1987), 250.

2. Ibid., 14.

3. Ibid., 15.

4. Ibid., 18.

5. Ibid., 8.

6. Myles Horton and Paulo Freire, *We Make the Road by Walking: Conversations on Education and Social Change*, eds. Brenda Bell, John Gaventa, and John Peters (Philadelphia: Temple University Press, 1990), 217.

7. Ibid.

8. Horton and Freire, *We Make the Road*, 61.

9. Linda Darling-Hammond, *The Right to Learn* (San Francisco: Jossey-Bass, 1997), 138..

10. Personal conversation, Fred Givens, Bronx Prep Charter School, New York City, August 2005.

11. Gleick, *Chaos*, 252.

12. Margaret Wheatley, *Leadership and the New Science* (San Francisco: Berrett-Kohler, 2006), 87.

13. Otto Scharmer, *Theory U: Leading From the Future as it Emerges* (Cambridge, MA: SOL, 2007), 36–37.

14. Scharmer, *Theory U*, 187.

15. Robert K. Greenleaf, *The Servant-Leader Within* (New York: Paulist Press, 2003), 71.

16. Wheatley, *Leadership and the New Science*, 131.

17. Thomas L. Friedman, *The World is Flat: A Brief History of the Twenty-First Century* (New York: Farrar, Straus & Giroux, 2005), 180.

18. Gleick, *Chaos*, 24.

19. Peter Senge, *The Fifth Discipline* (New York & London: Doubleday, 1990, 2006), 232.

20. Charles Haynes and Oliver Thomas, *Finding Common Ground: A Guide to Religious Liberty in Public Schools* (Nashville, TN: First Amendment Center, 2001), 62.

21. Ibid.

22. Horton and Freire, *We Make the Road*, 145.

23. Gleick, *Chaos*, 311.

Part II

PRACTICE

In part I, I outlined five skills that, taken together, provide an elastic framework for thinking about the art of collaborative leadership.

In part II, I want to give you a chance to test drive that framework, by way of the stories of three very different school communities that have tried, over several years, to establish fully developed democratic learning communities.

At the time this work took place, all three schools were part of a national initiative called the First Amendment Schools (FAS) project (www.firstamendmentschools.org). It is important to note that the schools, and the school leaders, were not doing their work with this book's framework in mind. Indeed, it is largely because of my experiences with these communities—and the countless conversations I had with dedicated, thoughtful educators, parents, and young people from across the country—that the framework from part I could come (with urgent patience) into being.

So, as you read the practices of part II, apply the theories of part I and see if they help you "see the whole board" of each school's journey. If it helps, you can also read with the following questions in mind:

- What are the most visible indicators of each school's organizational culture?
- What are the most invisible features of each school's organizational culture?
- If you could go back in time in each school's story and offer strategic advice, where in the story would you go, who would you speak to, and what would you advise? How might events unfold differently if your advice was heeded?
- If you could go back in time in each school's story and offer kudos, where in the story would you go, who would you congratulate, and why? How might have events unfolded differently if these actions were taken?

If you're interested in learning more about these schools, finding others like them, or sharing your own school's story, you can visit the Five Freedoms Network, an online global community of educators, students, and citizens who "share a commitment to First Amendment freedoms, democratic schools, and the idea that children deserve to be seen and heard."

A virtual public square for the twenty-first century, the Five Freedoms Network is made up of a growing list of members from different communities, perspectives, and points of interest. Join the conversation today—including an *American Schools* discussion group—at http://network.fivefreedoms.org.

Chapter Six

Fairview Elementary School
(Modesto, California)

Two Fairview students fill out their ballots in the school's first student council elections.

On a bright June morning in 2007, the five-year-old graduates of Fairview Elementary School's kindergarten classes impatiently adjust their homemade mortarboards and tassels. Each girl uses delicate hands to smooth out the ruffles of her princess dress, while the boys play with the colorful Mexican sashes stretched across their miniature suits.

As a teacher tests the sound system, the families of the young graduates settle into their seats. Overwhelmingly Latino, the crowd features a smattering of white, black, and Asian faces. Some adults are dressed in their Sunday finest. Others, heavily tattooed, wear t-shirts and jeans. All sit proudly, expectantly. Alongside the parents are older siblings, grandparents, and scores of even younger children. Squeals of delight at the colorful balloons mix with cries of discomfort and frustration, the hot sun of the central California valley already making its presence felt at this early hour.

As the ceremony begins, the children sing songs in both English and Spanish, and the video recorders start to roll. The children are taking the first step toward the reward that has brought their families here—a quality education. "This school is a place where we want all young people to have a voice," says Fairview's kinetic principal, Rob Williams, addressing the crowd. "We know, as your families do, that you are capable of great things."

For Williams, it is a chance to reflect on how far he and his school have come. Five years earlier, when the young people before him were just entering the world, Williams sparked a schoolwide experiment—to strengthen student engagement by making Fairview a more democratic place. Had it worked? Were they doing a better job of preparing the community's young people to succeed? In short, was Fairview a better place to work and learn than it had been five years ago?

✑

Fairview Elementary School sits at the end of Whitmore Avenue in Modesto, amid a confluence of several dusty back roads. Small houses with scorched lawns, homemade signs advertising cheap fresh produce, and row upon row of almond and walnut trees line the streets on this side of town—across the tracks from the privileged, scandal-breeding sanctuaries of Modesto's two most infamous residents, Scott Peterson and Gary Condit.

When Fairview opened in 1951, it was a small, one-building rural elementary school. Today it is responsible for more than 1,000 children, year-round, grades K through 6. Nearly 80 percent of its students are Latino. Many come from families whose parents are undocumented aliens. Almost all the students are poor; 86 percent qualify to receive Aid to Families with Dependent

Children (AFDC). Assessment data in 2006 showed 14 percent of students proficient in reading and 33 percent proficient in math.

On May 24, 2002, Williams kicked off the school year by publicly announcing that Fairview was adopting a clearer civic focus. With the help of a few teachers the previous fall, he submitted an application to become an inaugural member of the First Amendment Schools (FAS) project. Since March, when Williams learned the school was selected, he had been excitedly planning.

May 23, 2002

E-mail from Rob Williams

We have been working for two weeks in preparation for tomorrow's FAS Inauguration. We have planted patriotic flowers, painted rockets for our big ending, bought a patriotic cake for the FAS Task Force members and 800 red, white, and blue cookies for students ... the District painted the Fairview school sign and building trim. We have letters and certificates of recognition from our State Schools Superintendent, local assemblyman and senator and a letter from Senator Feinstein. The whole school is ABUZZ with excitement.

Fairview focused its rollout on physical reminders of the school's new civic mission. A sign in front of the school proclaimed Fairview a First Amendment School, listing all five freedoms prominently. Inside the campus, every hallway was given a street name that related to the ideas of democracy and freedom (Liberty Avenue, Constitution Boulevard, etc.). Visiting the office now meant visiting the West Wing. Walking through the central courtyard was a sojourn through Liberty Square. And checking out a book required a visit to the Library of Congress.

In conjunction with the new signs, Fairview revised its curriculum to include the Center for Civic Education's curricular materials, scope, and sequence. Thanks to its new street names, Fairview also implemented a mail-delivery system. Students were encouraged to write letters to each other, which were delivered daily during recess by the special education students. As teacher Chano Flores commented at the time, "We've already linked this behavior to our state standards. Our kids are reading and writing more than they ever have, and they're doing it because—first and foremost—it's fun for them."

Williams also decided to institute a new student government. Hope Carreno, a sunny young teacher already entering her thirteenth year at the school—she had never left since student teaching there—was placed in charge of the group. Once a week, she led thirty-five students, representing every homeroom across grades 1–6, through an agenda before helping them prepare to report back to their "constituencies." As they listened one afternoon, the legs of the youngest representatives dangled from their chairs, still a few feet from the ground.

To increase the opportunities for adult voice, Williams instituted regular town hall meetings where the goals of the school could be discussed. Toward the end of one meeting in November 2002, he asked a few of the Latino parents, silent up to this point because of their limited language skills, if they had anything they would like to add. One spoke tentatively about her gratitude to the school for its parent classes; another said she was thankful for the differences she had noticed in her kids.

The final parent to speak, a young woman holding an infant, told the group she and other concerned Fairview parents recently decided to launch a petition drive. Growing in animation and passion as she spoke, she read the text of the petition:

> Conscious of our rights under the First Amendment to the Constitution of the United States, while realizing that our children's school has been designated a First Amendment School, we are petitioning for a redress of grievances and worries that we have.

The parents went on to explain in respectful Spanish that random passersby could too easily enter the classrooms at the front of the school. "So far, no serious incidents have occurred," the parents wrote, "but we would prefer that action occur before anything tragic happens to our children. For that reason, we ask for your cooperation in the construction of a fence in front of the school."

Although the petition campaign was just a week old, nearly eighty parents had signed it. The woman explained she had gotten the idea from the new sign in front of the school. "When I saw the sign go up," she said, "I knew we had rights and we were being asked to use them." Williams smiled widely. "That's what I hoped would happen. I wanted anyone who arrived at our school to know that this was a place where we took freedom seriously."

Because Williams supported the parent petition, it was taken seriously at the district office. A few months later, the new fence was built.

As a consequence of this early success, a group of Latino parents launched a new parent organization—*Padres Con Voz* (Parents with a Voice). Before long, Vice Principal Cecilia Cobb, who is bilingual, was charged with staffing monthly meetings with the group. The discussions had a UN flair to them—the monolingual parents wore small earpieces, through which bilingual teacher Richard Braun provided them with a running translation.

By the spring of 2003, another schoolwide challenge had emerged: a growing desire on the part of some students, teachers, and parents to do away with the school's uniform policy. Williams was pleased to find another opportunity for the school to practice its newfound commitment to civil debate. With the help of a few hand-selected teachers, he organized a special assembly, to which the entire community was invited. "We decided to have one student, one teacher, and one parent speak on behalf of both sides of the issue, and then let the community decide the issue by a vote." In the end, by a narrow margin, the school decided to do away with its uniform policy—a decision the school district supported.

In addition to the schoolwide changes, many of Fairview's teachers began adopting a different approach to classroom management. Deborah Supnet, a veteran teacher at Fairview, explained the changes this way: "I got rid of hand raising in my class. Instead, I teach the children to listen for when the other child stops talking." Others took advantage of the school's focus to acquire relevant professional development from the National Paideia Center, a North Carolina–based organization that specializes in helping teachers conduct Socratic seminars.

In all, 2003 had been a transformational year. "I have NEVER had a school year like this," Williams wrote in a June e-mail. "I am still on fire because the mood and culture at Fairview has changed. We were packed to the gills with parents at graduation. And now the Union reps are in my office working

---

July 20, 2003

E-mail from teacher Suzi Tornberg

My class is still using the petition system this year. I informed the class on Monday that the last 15 minutes of the day will be reserved as study hall time to complete any last minute homework while I'm still there to help. Wednesday two students asked for a petition discussion. The class president led the discussion. The petition asked for the last 15 minutes to be free P.E. time outside. After clarifying questions and comments, the class voted. The outcome was 15-17 that we would not have free P.E. time and that we would keep our study hall time. Democracy works if we are willing to give it a chance!

August 15, 2003

E-mail from teacher Liz Benson

I thought the Town Hall meeting went very well yesterday. Chano and Richard did a great job. It was a good idea for teachers to take the leadership role at the meeting. The ideas and concerns were well thought out and were shared often. It was exciting to see parents, students, and teachers sharing ideas. I thought all voices were heard. The parents understood that without their support in education, we will not have the future leaders they want. The action plan for our second year based on this information will be more powerful and more supported by the parents, students, and many teachers.

together brainstorming how to resolve a staffing issue. There is a new spirit of seeking common ground. It is the way schools should work."

Against this backdrop of deliberative successes, Fairview, like every other school in the district, was equally preoccupied with its student-achievement data—and how to improve it. "We've been struggling for the last ten years to get good results," Williams explained, "and figure out how to get students, teachers, and principals to be motivated and more accountable to each other.

"At Fairview, our big issue is getting our English Language Learners to do well on a state test that's in English. The kids have traditionally not done well in grades 3–6 on the reading section of the English Language Arts test from the state. The percentages have been the pattern for the last five years. So my district is looking to me and others on my side of town to figure out what we're going to do to improve the test scores of our English Language Learners."

Between 2002 and 2004, Fairview had seen steady growth in its student achievement data (see table 6.1). For Williams, this mission was not enough. "At Fairview we take seriously the social, affective, and civic development of all the kids, to a point that we have a dual mission—civic and academic. I think they're closely linked. We've been monitoring how our kids feel about empathy, caring for others, how government works, city council works. That's just part of our conversations in school."

Table 6.1 Base API—Fairview Elementary School

	2002	2003	2004
Schoolwide	623	638	643
Hispanic	604	628	634
Socioeconomic	602	621	626
English Learner	No data	No data	No data

In September 2004, some of Fairview's teachers were asked to describe any changes they'd witnessed in the school. "These kids definitely know more about rights and responsibilities in comparison to my last school," said the new media teacher. A smiling young deputy in charge of school security agreed. "At recess here, kids have petitions for everything—ravioli, tetherballs, the playground. I've been in plenty of schools, but I've never seen that before."

When the teachers who predate Rob's tenure spoke, the sentiment shifted. "Believe me, everyone knows we're a First Amendment School," said one kindergarten teacher. She didn't mean it as a compliment. "The concepts we're being asked to share with the children, especially the topics for the schoolwide assemblies, are all above—way above—my kids. It's going to be nearly impossible for them to sit still. I think we should have K–3 assemblies at one time and 4–6 assemblies at another."

Rob, sitting nearby, responded quickly—"That's a great idea"—but it was clear the teacher was not convinced. She smiled curtly, stood up, and left.

Later that afternoon, a different group of Fairview teachers were asked to rank the quality of faculty voice at their school. Several teachers shot knowing glances at each other. How candid should we be, they seemed to be asking each other.

Some simply had too much to say to remain silent. "I guess things are getting better, and people are getting more comfortable going to Rob," said one teacher. "But many of us still don't feel like we have a voice." A third-grade teacher agreed. "We need more collaborative possibilities here, and less being told what to do. We never even knew the paperwork to become a First Amendment School was filed," she said. "It would be nice if he came into our grade-level meetings and met with us. He'd see that we're not against him and that he can trust us. He must trust us."

"There's a lot of quasi-choice here," a kindergarten teacher added. "And he's almost there, in terms of giving us a choice, but the decisions feel like they've already been made. It's like he poses the questions but there isn't really any question about what we're going to do." Several heads nodded in affirmation. "Just this Monday at our faculty meeting," added another teacher, "he told us, 'I'm the principal and that's how it's going to be done.'"

Later, Rob explained a new program he hoped would improve the quality of communication among colleagues. "Our district is heavily unionized, so we put aside $25,000 for substitutes so we could have at least twice-a-month meetings. We call it the Teachers' Café, where rotating subs come through and release teachers in ninety-minute blocks to talk to each other. The scheduling of this time to talk has been a huge way for me to get to the school's goals and also to get to my own personal agenda about creating a democratic school."

The day ends with a schoolwide assembly at which twenty-eight student-council candidates deliver their campaign speeches. The advent of student government is an exciting new aspect of the school, but it's still an uneven process. The students learned a week ago that they'd have to give a speech and it shows; the whole affair seems rushed.

Still, the students are inspiring. "I would like to make knowing two languages cool," says one candidate for president. "I would help people to not get in trouble in school," says one boy. A young blond girl vows to "always try to do my best, even if I feel like being lazy." Unable to follow the content, the kindergartners still appreciate the chance to heartily yell "Bravo!" at the end of each speech.

January 9, 2004

E-mail from Rob Williams

Is there daily and weekly evidence of our vision? This question is always with me. I get frustrated not seeing daily civic lessons, and students engaged in "real" conversations about feelings, school and current events. If I could change classroom practices with a magic wand it would be that tomorrow I see this type of daily civic engagement... but, it will happen!!!

At our Monday staff meeting we are having a family talk! Just two questions to answer: What is helping you feel successful? What is hindering you from feeling successful? Teachers will be asked to answer questions from a District, School or Classroom level. All answers will be shared. At the follow-up meeting on January 26, we will review the teacher responses...we will protect those items that help, work on problems and accept some issues as non-negotiable. And then we will have a more personal conversation about our Moral Purpose for doing this work, what is our shared vision and values, and what do we as a school want to accomplish. Should be good!

The next morning, sixty members of the Fairview community accept the school's open invitation to attend a brainstorming session. There are familiar faces—Rob, Richard Braun, Chano Flores, Cecilia Cobb—but there are also parents, members of the Modesto Rotary Club, principals and teachers from other community schools, and even the editor of the *Modesto Bee*. Most important, every student who gave a campaign speech the day before has been invited. Arriving in their best clothes, the candidates quickly form an imposing line at the breakfast buffet table. To be eight and get free muffins—it doesn't get much better than that.

After Rob asks people in the room to introduce themselves, the Fairview team presents a PowerPoint review of the previous year. Establishing a student government. Integrating civics throughout the curriculum. Building a radio station. It's a meaty list, and the core team members radiate pride in their accomplishments.

The meeting ends with the presenters sharing their preliminary year-two action plans, asking the audience to react and offer revisions or new suggestions. It turns out to be a rich exchange. A young father named Jorge suggests that some part of the action plans be focused on addressing the segregated parent groups at the school. "Right now there's *Padres Con Voz*, and there's the PTA group (whose members are almost entirely white), and it seems like the two parent groups have two different missions." Armando Flores, a candidate for the city council, suggests a plan be dedicated to the work of "passing it on, and passing it around," whereby other local schools could get a newsletter providing updates of the best work at Fairview and how to get more involved. Laura Malagon, a parent volunteer and community pillar, asks for more to be done with the media. "We need to share these goals with the entire community, and we're missing a big opportunity to do that." When Rob points to the editor of the *Modesto Bee*, Laura smiles but continues. "That's important, but we also need to publicize this work in the Spanish newspapers."

Finally one of the students—a quiet vice presidential candidate named Diana Lee—raises her hand, walks to the podium, and offers a sincere thanks. "I'm just grateful that of all the kids in the school, I could come today and be a part of this wonderful experience. It's very important that we get a voice because sometimes schools don't even listen to kids, but kids should have a say in what their school looks like." The room erupts in applause.

By the end of the exchange, Fairview has four recommendations for its year-three action plans:

1. to improve communication between and among the staff;
2. to improve communication between and among the different communities;

January 16, 2004

E-mail from Rob Williams, Fairview Elementary School

I have been thinking what evidence that the FAS Project is making a difference in the life of a school and district. And, it is EVIDENT.

The Fairview staff is so "unified." We are planning next steps to take the staff to the next level of Team building. The next meeting is asking staff what is their passion for teaching and to bring an artifact that represents their passion. We will share our collective passion before talking about a collective vision, purpose, and values. WHICH INCLUDES RAMPING UP THEIR COMMITMENT TO CREATING DEMOCRATIC CLASSROOMS.

3. to unify the parent organizations under one umbrella; and
4. to institutionalize the link between individual rights and civic responsibilities at the school.

As the group files out, Diana approaches a visitor and recites the forty-five words of the First Amendment by heart—she has been asked to do so at a patriotic assembly later that fall. The visitor wishes her luck on the elections, slated for later that day. "Thank you," she says politely. "I just hope I win."

❧

By the start of the 2006–2007 school year, Fairview had already spent four years working to become a more democratic place. Partly as a result, its student API data had continued to improve (see table 6.2). The school had put together a leadership team of administrators and teachers and invested in training for the group around core issues like leadership, analyzing data, and how to conduct grade-level meetings.

Fairview had also become a national news story. Rob, Laura Malagon, and a group of students appeared on the cover of *Social Education*. The school was featured in the *Modesto Bee* several times. Wisconsin Public Television produced a special episode about the school. *Reader's Digest* featured the school in a special profile. So did the *Washington Post*.

One part of the school that drew a lot of the media attention—student government—was still alive and well at Fairview, although Hope Carreno was no longer a part of it. Asked to reflect on how the school had changed, she of-

Table 6.2   Base API—Fairview Elementary School

	2002	2003	2004	2005	2006
Schoolwide	623	638	643	651	678
Hispanic	604	628	634	646	670
Socioeconomic	602	621	626	628	665
English Learner	No data	No data	No data	618	653

fered a mixed review. "When we first started this work everyone thought Rob was out for himself," she began. "But then we got selected, and we started to think, 'Maybe we can make a difference.' At first, it was a lot of fun. But then it became too much work.

"It's like once the official excitement wore off, people started getting jealous of each other and wondering why certain people got chosen to do certain things. It started to feel like some people got preferential treatment. Then the town hall meetings stopped, and I think we stopped being as democratic. It's like he went from dictating to deliberating and then back to dictating."

Another teacher, Bee Yang, saw things differently. "Before we adopted this focus, it was like we were walking on a cloud—we were not as focused," said Yang, a seven-year veteran of Fairview. "I didn't use to see a lot of parents, especially the Hispanic parents. But our staff is more focused now. Before, if we had a staff meeting, we'd be all over the place. We're more goal-oriented now. Our student government is so much stronger now. And when it comes to important issues, we always discuss them."

April 20, 2005

Local TV Coverage of Ice Cream Truck Petition

MODESTO, Calif. -- Students at a Modesto school are banding together with a campaign to keep ice cream trucks from selling BB guns after one of their own was suspended for bringing a BB gun to school.

The issue started when 11-year-old Santiago Sanchez brought a BB gun to Fairview Elementary School after purchasing it from a ice cream truck vendor. Sanchez was busted for bringing the gun to school.

"Immediately, he was taken away from the classroom. Without further word, he was suspended for five days," said teacher Nick Kellner.

Sanchez said he wondered why it was so easy for children to buy toy guns from ice cream trucks.

"I saw the BB gun. I asked him how much did it cost. He said $5, and he sold it to me," Sanchez said.

So far, three students at Fairview Elementary School have been suspended in cases related to the BB guns. And two students have been hit by BBs.

Now, all of Santiago's fifth-grade class is rallying around him to try to ban the sale of toy guns to children. The students started "project citizen," putting together a petition and picket signs in preparation for a two-day protest against ice cream vendors next week.

"To not buy BB guns because it is pretty dangerous. To make the ice cream man stop because lots of people could buy them. They could just hurt each other," said student Sergio Esparza.

The plan is to turn the ban on toy guns into a citywide ordinance.

"We bring it to the city council. We see if the public policy becomes something more," Kellner said.

Stanislaus County Sheriff's Department deputy and school resource officer Justin Ownbey said that if caught, ice cream truck drivers could face criminal charges.

"Any BB device, toy gun, anything that shoots out a little projectile is considered an imitation fire arm. And the sale of that to a minor without parent consent is a misdemeanor," Ownbey said.

Authorities said that 11-year-old Leela Lowe was hit by a BB while playing in her neighborhood. She said she doesn't want to it to happen to anyone else.

"When they sell the guns, kids just buy them like they are nothing. They just shoot people with it," Lowe said.

Students plan to take the school's civic mission to the city council sometime next month.

Balbina Rodriguez, a third-year teacher who left her previous career as an accountant to help address what she saw as the growing gap "between the haves and the have-nots," struck more of a middle ground. "Our strength is empowering students," she said. "That's why I came here. And I think the kids still feel that way. You can see that they have better visions for their future now."

Rodriguez was less positive about the adults. "I think we need to go back and look at what we did the first two years. Our commitment to equality and voice was so much stronger. We always talked about how to instill a sense of rights and responsibilities in everyone. But somehow that spirit died out a bit."

On the eve of the kindergarten graduation in 2007, Rob considered the strengths and weaknesses of his school, five years after becoming a First Amendment School. "I'm in the throes of a huge leadership change in how I manage," he explained. "Our district model has changed as well. It used to be more top-down, where the superintendent and my other bosses were telling us what to do. But now we have more accountability at each school site. A year ago, the district would have said, 'This is your accountability plan.' This year, we took about six months to develop our own site accountability plan. We set up grade-level meetings, decided how we would monitor our progress, and we're still getting results.

"In some ways, this is because we've become a more collaborative place. And yet I also find myself becoming more assertive. It's both, I guess—I've become more assertive and more deliberative.

"I firmly believe that a school based on the guiding principles of individual freedom and shared voice makes a difference," he said. "I see now that a school community can instill in students a deep respect for differences, a commitment to each other, and the willingness to learn how to deal with conflict. I also recognize that before this process, we had no norms for how we talked to each other. I'm proud that we've been working on trying to build a learning community and a spirit of collaboration between grade levels. Though the structures were there, it wasn't until the last year and a half that we said, 'No, these are our norms.' Then I started trying to model it, where people could say, 'I think this is not going to work for me' and I would really listen. And now, the norms go beyond me. Before, there was dissension, disagreement, and union battles. Now, the idea of collaboration and team building is ingrained at our school."

Then Rob shared a recent comment a teacher had made to him. "'You've lost your civic-minded vision for this school,' she told me. 'I don't believe we're a First Amendment School any more.' I see that as a huge problem. And she's not wrong—I feel a bit like Jekyll and Hyde right now.

"I think preparing kids for the test is critical for success. But for the last five years I have been asking teachers, 'How do we make kids feel connected to school? How do we make sure kids pass on to the next grade level, and have a voice in the school?' That, to me, is what principals should be doing.

"I think unless I carry the torch, with this whole shift in our school, our focus will be lost and I need to bring it back. There are pockets in my school

March 31, 2006

E-mail from Rob Williams

Since January 2006, I feel like our school is "lost in translation." It seems that we have lost our rudder. In California the immigration issue is hot. But, at Fairview it is hidden and not open to debate. Damn disappointing. I notified staff about good resources to talk about immigration and to encourage debate. I'll see next week. I plan to sponsor a debate for grades 5-6.

where teachers, if I were gone tomorrow, would run civic-minded and democratic classrooms. But there's just been a falloff in the time we've spent talking together and planning together. I really think the school has lost its sense of living out our shared vision.

"When the *Washington Post* called me, the writer hit me with questions like, 'What does it mean to have a school with a civic mission? What does it look like? Why are you different than somebody else?' It made me feel good that people outside the school want to hear about those things, to feel like schools should be doing something for kids and adults that is meaningful. Yet the next week when I sat down with my superintendent, he's wasn't asking me, 'What civic-minded activity are your kids working on? Which of your grade levels has the strongest knowledge of democratic principles?'

"Some might argue that's not the role of schools, but it sure does feel good to have kids, especially in my population, who can say, 'I understand how the court system works, and if I was upset about a problem in my neighborhood, I would know what to do. I'm going to take my mom and my grandparent and we're going to go to the school board meeting or city council meeting. We're going to debate and get a resolution to the problem.'

"It frustrates me to no end that we've lost that conversation, lost that focus. I feel really fulfilled that people want to hear a principal say that schools should be about academics and about having a public purpose. But I'm not sure we have that same strong sense we had before, the belief that we've got something really special happening at our school. As soon as the cameras are gone, I don't know how real it is anymore. I just don't think the depth is there; it's not as intense and long term as I'd like. I wish my school was on fire all the time.

"Still, I think the solution is simply not to give up. If we give some time to let kids talk about and understand the Pledge of Allegiance, that's strong learning. We just have to get back to continuing the conversation and making sure people are aware of what we value.

"And yet I recognize it's all for naught unless I have good test results. It just doesn't matter how civic minded I am, so that's why I feel like I'm Jekyll and Hyde sometimes. I need to show that a school that is really focused on its civic purpose can also get good results.

"If you look at my behavior as an administrator five years ago versus today and you ask people what's the difference I think they would say Rob is much more patient about listening to concerns and much more collaborative in making decisions looking for consensus. I think there's been a huge shift in the culture of the school and building capacity within each other about how we work together and make decisions.

"Still, the challenges keep coming. I've been at this school for seven years and I feel like a whole new generation of families is coming through. I feel a huge disconnect with them. I think people respect me for having been here a long time, but I don't have a close relationship with many of my new dads and moms. Plus, we're struggling with our PTA. We have a new PTA and we have a charter but we've been fighting. Our *Padres Con Voz* group, which was a really active parent advocacy group, just fell apart when one of the leaders left and went to another school district. And now I think community expectation for my school and my school's needs is zilch. Parents drive their cars and drop their kids off, pick them up, and that's about the whole extent of involvement.

"I know my community wants to help its children and get more involved with school, but the problem is I don't have enough support staff. I've been able to convince people to allocate money to build a structure to help ongoing meetings with parents. In terms of priorities or money, bridging a relationship with community has not been important.

"When you talk about shared norms and values, lots of people agree that being civic minded and having a public purpose is good, but we're too busy getting kids ready for the test."

Rob's eyes darted about as he spoke, his passion and restlessness evident. "My leadership goal is to demonstrate through my actions that I'm doing what is best for my students and for my site. It's being assertive and being firm about my decisions. I just had to practice this yesterday and I said I'm not going to compromise. My ability to lead this school depends upon sticking to this decision. I'm expecting people to work harder and that we're going to be more civic minded. I've been here seven years so I know I don't have much time left, but I think even if I went to another school I would carry that spirit of listening, but I'm the principal and we're going to get it done right.

"We'll just need to see what happens next."

Chapter Seven

Nursery Road Elementary School (Irmo, South Carolina)

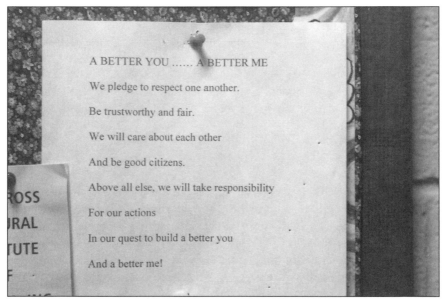

One of Nursery Road's Kindergarten Constitutions *is displayed on a teacher's bulletin board.*

In July 2005, a reporter for the *State* newspaper in Columbia, South Carolina, asked a number of local elementary school children why America celebrates the Fourth of July.

Most of the answers were predictably personal. "So we can eat hot dogs," said one. "Because we get to watch fireworks," said another. One child thought the entire country celebrated the Fourth of July because it was his brother's birthday.

A fourth grader from Nursery Road Elementary School, Vante Lee, gave an answer that was noticeably different. "We celebrate the 4th of July because we celebrate freedom and the chance to make our own decisions."

Vante's clarity about the purpose of Independence Day was indicative of the culture his school had created, beginning in 2002 when Principal Mary Kennerly decided to strengthen Nursery Road's commitment to democratic principles. In the years that followed, the southern school would receive national attention for its work, its students would travel around the country sharing what they had learned, and educators were asking, "What is happening at Nursery Road?"

Five years after that work began, the landscape at Nursery Road had changed markedly. Kennerly was no longer the principal, the school was no longer interested in labeling itself a First Amendment School, and community members spoke of both student empowerment and stifled adult voices.

What happened during those five years, and what lessons could be learned from the experience?

∽≼✦≽∽

Nursery Road is a K–5 school located in the Lexington 5 district in Irmo, a bedroom community in suburban Columbia. The school, which opened in 1980 to accommodate a growing student population in the district that resulted from "white flight" from the newly integrated city schools, works hard to serve its increasingly diverse population well.

There is much evidence to suggest Nursery Road is a high-functioning school. Student art brightens every hallway. The school's numerous awards are displayed at several locations around the building. Many of the teachers who opened Nursery Road in 1980 remain on the faculty today. Former students now teach alongside colleagues who taught them. And significant numbers of parents can always be found in the school, volunteering their time.

On a September day in 2002, this number was doubtless inflated given the school's determination to build the world's largest American flag from some 2,800 cup cakes—a flag to be visited by classes on the morning of Citizenship Day (September 17) and eaten by the students during lunch.

Mary Kennerly, Nursery Road's longtime principal, stands at the front of the school, cheerfully greeting visitors. A mother and grandmother, Mary has long brown curly hair, colored glasses, and a conciliatory voice. As she invites her guests to enter the building, her dangly earrings jingle in concert to her body movements. It is clear she has high hopes for the school's newly articulated focus on democratic principles and student voice.

We are escorted to the science lab, where the room is set for a full day meeting of the school's leadership team, augmented by parents, community members, and representatives of the community's middle and high schools. As people settle into their seats with Styrofoam cups of tepid coffee, Mary begins to facilitate a morning discussion framed by two questions:

1. What do we want our students to know and be able to do?
2. What do we want our community to know and be able to do?

The self-selected group approaches the questions—and the school's newly adopted emphasis on founding principles—with great enthusiasm. As one parent boasts, "We bleed red, white, and blue here." Before lunch, the group identifies three goal statements:

- All students will participate in grade-level appropriate activities that teach, model, and apply First Amendment principles and promote democratic citizenship.
- A student government that represents all students and provides opportunities for them to practice citizenship will be reconstituted.
- The community will be engaged in implementing the First Amendment Schools project.

The next day, Citizenship Day, finds all special guests on a tightly orchestrated visit to nearly every classroom in the school. Time is also allocated for each grade-level team to discuss their understanding of the school's involvement in the First Amendment Schools (FAS) project with FAS representatives.

In the classrooms, students in grades two through five talk and read about their First Amendment freedoms. After lunch, a schoolwide assembly is held in the student activity forum. It begins with a parade of flags of all the countries represented by the families of the student body. The school choir sings numerous patriotic songs, while some students dressed as historical figures—James Madison, Frederick Douglass, and Susan B. Anthony, to name a few—give patriotic speeches. One student asks a visitor from Washington, D.C., if he works for the president and asks him to say hello.

After school that day, a faculty meeting is convened, at which teachers are asked to react to the draft goal statements and help brainstorm additional action steps. Working in small groups in the cafeteria, the faculty generates some new ideas for the FAS team to consider. Only one teacher forgets to wear the designated red, white, and blue.

Eighteen months later, over she crab soup, a BBQ sandwich, and collard greens, a Nursery Road parent wants to talk to me about Mary. "This is a remarkable place," she begins, "and it all begins with our principal. The key is that she's so patient, so that when she presents something new to the faculty, she never presses them. Sometimes that means it may take three years before the teachers decide they want to go forward with the idea, but that's why our community support is so high."

The next morning, as a colleague and I tour the hallways and meet with teachers by grade level, several teachers admit that, at first, they thought the FAS project sounded daunting for elementary-aged kids. "I didn't think many of my kids could say [the First Amendment], let alone memorize it," says one fifth-grade teacher. "I was in shock when I first heard about this," adds another. Several confess that their first thought was, "Here we go—one more thing."

"But," a third-grade teacher continues, "this project is one of the best things we've done at Nursery Road. I see now how fundamental it is to what we're doing. Now when my kids say the First Amendment, they actually know what it means. It's so exciting to see how much they've internalized it."

Many teachers choose to speak about specific projects at the school, such as the decision to reinstitute student government. "The best thing we did was have all the kids—even the kindergartners—watch the taped speeches each candidate had to deliver. They were really listening. I can't wait to see how we build on this next year." At this point, Mary offers her own observations. "I think we gained a lot from our decision to require each candidate to spend some time after school learning about how to deliver a speech—and to insist that parents attend the workshops too. Those parents made sure they were there for their kids, including some parents who don't usually get involved. And the word spread from there. They may not have been learning directly about the First Amendment, but they learned how to get involved at the school. And I think that trust will continue to carry over for us."

A teacher then relates a story about a particular parent, the mother of a sometimes-difficult young boy named Roger. "Roger's mom was cursing us out in August for this or that, and now she's saying she wants him to stay at school longer. And we've had lots of other kids begging to stay after school. It's impossible to measure how much that's mattered to our larger sense of community."

Later that morning, at a schoolwide assembly, we get our first sense of what the teachers were talking about. Each newly elected student officer takes a public oath of duty. Instead of the Bible, small hands are placed on top of important Nursery Road documents, like the school's mission statement and discipline code. With solemn, proud expressions, each child publicly pledges to "use responsibility in all decision-making, and in the exercise of all freedoms."

The assembly concludes with student work that deals more directly with the First Amendment. Five third-graders deliver a PowerPoint presentation of a book they produced, "The Loss of the First Amendment," a cautionary tale about what happens when the president returns from breakfast one day to discover that the First Amendment is missing. Order cannot be restored until a South Carolina child hears about the chaos in Washington and reminds the president what the First Amendment really states. In the interim, the country had been operating under a "messed up" version that stated: "Congress shall not make a law respecting a reestablishment of legends, of pressing the un-free execute thereof; or a vision of teaching, or of the test, or the might of the people to loudly resemble, and to audition the government for a red dress of grievances."

The assembly ends with everyone singing the "First Amendment Song." Sung to the tune of 'When the Saints go Marching In," the tune features stanzas like, "Oh yes we love / the rights we have, Oh yes we love / the rights we have, And we'll defend / the rights of others, Oh yes we love / the rights we have."

Later that afternoon, after a second assembly at which the school has a chance to ask questions of the Honorable Jean Toll, the first female chief justice of the State Supreme Court, I sit down with Mary to reflect on Nursery Road's first year. "We need to address the issue of neutrality with teachers among students," she says. "Lots of people down here still feel victimized by the federal government since Reconstruction, so there are adults who feel it's their duty to impose their will on young people." Mary adds she has yet to extend the project deeply into the community, "because as a faculty we haven't yet congealed. We still need to make sure everyone in the building understands what this project is really *about*, before we extend any further."

The next morning—May 16, 2003—we arrive to watch Nursery Road's TV announcements and participate in the schoolwide (and state-mandated) moment of silence. Afterward we push tables together and form a square around which all FAS team members can sit for a strategy session.

To no one's surprise, Mary has a plan. After helping ourselves to coffee, juice, trail mix, and mini bagels, we are handed tidy blue folders with an outline for the day; on one side are supplementary materials about the project—the FAS vision statement, a project activity checklist, and so on; on the other side are Nursery Road's planning documents from the year—its project-related action plans and a summary of activities completed.

Once the general conversation starts, Spanish teacher BonnieJean Avilez sets the tone. "There are so many moments to celebrate," she said. "I just feel so privileged and I want to spread that feeling to other schools." PTA president Sherry Satterwhaite adds that she "keep[s] trying to give but I get back so much more every time." Fourth grade teacher Harriet Hamilton offers a more specific reflection: "The First Amendment activities allow kids to excel in multiple intelligence areas." And kindergarten teacher Judy Tinder says, "Next year, we'll have the little kids vote again but this time we'll tell them why their vote doesn't really count yet."

Judy is responding to a question from the day before, when she first described the elections and mentioned how much fun her kids had had. When she added that their votes didn't count, I asked why. Her answer made sense from a developmental perspective, and yet clearly the question stuck. "In fact," she continues, "what if we registered third graders to vote from now on, as a way to indicate the importance and responsibility associated with the privilege?" Then media specialist Sarah Sheely jumps into the conversation. "That's a great idea," she says. "We could even have the high schoolers come to us to register the little kids, while we send the little kids to register them. That way we can reinforce at both levels the notion of being ready to enter a new stage of responsibility."

A discussion of civic responsibilities eventually turns to a discussion of individual rights, something the group feels less comfortable with. How would people react if majority perspectives were publicly challenged? Harriet speaks first. "As adults, we all need to make sure we respect all kids and make all perspectives safe for sharing." BonnieJean is less sure. "I do wonder how much control we still feel the need to cling to. I think we really need to look into that as a First Amendment School."

Then Sherry takes the hypothetical a bit further. "What will we do if book protests start?" She looks worried. Mary calmly suggests that the group "provide parent education on dealing with different opinions now, so we can teach everyone the value of their children learning different opinions before any conflicts break out. We need to convey the need to be responsible for the rights of others, especially when we're in the majority." The group brainstorms some possible avenues—a newsletter, a handbook, a special event via the PTA—for educating their parent community. "Being a First Amendment

School really helps us to introduce these topics," Harriet shares. "It opens up more opportunities to talk about these issues."

With lunchtime approaching, the conversation is briefly interrupted by a visit from the four student government leaders. Looking nervous and a little stunned, they take their seats and begin to offer a report of what they feel are the main issues at the school. "We need to play more games during instruction," says a thin wisp of a girl named Nidha. "Maybe a litter clean-up contest," offers Emma. "More sports teams," says Samuel, "and we should get rid of the assigned seating rule at lunch."

Samuel's last suggestion prompts a wave of constructive adult advice. One teacher explains that the main reason for the assigned seating rule is so no child will be left alone with no one to sit with at lunch. "What would you say to that young child if no one were sitting with him?" she asks. The first response is honest and direct. "Tough luck," says Nidha, already a grizzled veteran of the battle trenches of youth survival.

On my way out of the school, one teacher insists I see what some teachers and parents have done to the cafeteria that morning. To honor the students for finishing their state tests, the school is sponsoring a Mardi Gras celebration. We reach the cafeteria, where the walls have been covered with purple and green streamers, giant paintings of actors or jugglers, and signs for a special seating area. Immaculate, colorful tablecloths, bottles of soda, and theatrical masks complete the scene. Nearby, a sound system provides the music; a dance floor is nearby. Posted guidelines say things like "Wear masks if you want," and "Have fun!"

I walk into the dining area, and again I find Sherry Satterwhaite, this time filling bowls with popcorn. She sees me and smiles, beaming. "Isn't this wonderful?"

❦

On Friday, August 8, 2004, I returned to Nursery Road Elementary School for a full day of FAS activities. NRES teachers, still used to the later wake-up privileges of the summer months, slowly entered the school auditorium at 7:45 A.M. to the sounds of a "Celebrate Diversity" DVD Mary had bought during her time in Washington earlier that summer. Colleagues paid little attention to the images, choosing instead to swap summer vacation stories or share new ideas for the fall.

At 8:00 A.M. sharp, Mary began the day with a brief overview, followed by a series of FAS celebrations from the past year. She spoke of the third grade class that produced "The Loss of the First Amendment," praised the teachers who developed a First Amendment curriculum for the book *The Landry News*, and shared memories from the most recent FAS Leadership meeting in July, which five members of the community had attended. Kindergarten teacher Judy Tinder offered her own testimonial—"I've been here twenty-six years," she said, "and I've been on a lot of committees. But this is the first time I've begged Mary to actually let me stay *on* one of them."

After spending a few minutes on celebrations, each teacher received a yellow folder with their name and a set of materials for the day. The materials ranged from relevant articles or recommended resources to a brief summary of the school's FAS-related accomplishments from the previous year. Since Mary's chief focus for the teachers that day related to community outreach, there was also a white sheet of paper each teacher would be asked to complete later. One simple directive stretched across its top. "Community members will know and be able to do—."

Mary first asked the faculty to complete a FAS checklist, so everyone could get a sense of what Nursery Road might look like as a more fully developed First Amendment School. Next, she asked the group to work together to generate some shared expectations for the school's new student government. "It's important that we share a language," she said, "when thinking about issues of school governance. So we need to formalize our expectations in terms of self-, classroom-, and schoolwide-governance issues."

To help the group arrive at a useful conclusion, the exercise was framed around the following question: "What is it we want our students to learn about self-governance?" Teachers met in their grade teams and worked in small groups to generate a list of goal statements and then reported their findings to the large group. "We need to teach our children to think for themselves," said the kindergarten teachers. "Too often they do whatever the people around them are doing, so we need to figure out a way to make them less afraid to think for themselves." A number of other ideas were shared, including:

- "We want our kids to learn how to accept consequences better."
- "We need to teach them the difference between having a vote and stating a preference, so they can understand that voting is so important because it *changes* things."
- "We need to teach them how to recognize how their behavior affects others, so they can learn how to be more responsible."

For the final exercise, Mary asked each group to think about how they might accomplish these goals. One teacher imagined a video brief for the school's Friday TV show, in which two adults go about solving a dispute the wrong way. Two students would then be brought in to show the adults how to resolve their conflict based on First Amendment principles. A teacher from the first grade team said his group wanted to use the principles from Roxanne

Kriete's book *Morning Meeting* "to make our classes more like democratic communities." As the teachers shared their thoughts, members of the administrative team took detailed notes.

Then Mary directed the teachers to a series of bulletin boards at the back of the cafeteria. Each had different key words written across the top of large pieces of paper. Mary directed them to one that asked the teachers to determine what kinds of decisions they would be comfortable turning over to the students. "Please write down your thoughts at some point before we reconvene after lunch," she asked.

Later that day, Mary looked at the list. Generally, it reflected cautiousness on the part of the teachers. Whereas one supported the idea of students helping her produce class rules and consequences, the others were willing to empower students to decide four things: when to speak in class; which topics to research; what they want for lunch; and what to write about for essays. "Our teachers may be more reluctant than I thought," Mary confessed.

A year later—August 2005—at the annual meeting of the National Conference of State Legislatures (NCSL) in Seattle, five Nursery Road students gave a keynote presentation to some of the 7,000 or so state legislators attending the conference.

Founded in 1975 "with the conviction that legislative service is one of democracy's worthiest pursuits," NCSL had convened policymakers from all fifty states with the theme, "Strong States, Strong Nation." The day before the student presentation, Bill Gates had opened the meeting with a speech to a capacity crowd.

Waiting backstage in the green room before their speech, the students— nine-year-old Will Bowman and ten-year-olds Joshua Jenkins, Madelyn Hazslett, Pooja Mulhotra, and Miller Love—seemed blissfully unaware of any need to feel nervous. Their parents were another story. Strategically placed in the front row of the giant ballroom, they paced anxiously back and forth, rehearsing their children's lines with near-religious fervor while their kids playfully crammed themselves into a small couch, energized by the sugar from their complimentary cans of soda. When they learned Bill Gates had sat in the same couch just a few days earlier, the students rifled through the gaps in the cushions, certain they would find ample change.

A few moments later, it was show time.

"Can you name the five freedoms listed in the First Amendment?" asked Miller. "Can you name all of the freedoms in the Bill of Rights and in each of the other amendments?"

"Some of you can," Will added, "because it is part of your job. But three years ago *none* of us knew the freedoms in the First Amendment. The teachers didn't know them and the principal didn't *even* know them. Now we all know them—even the principal and the kindergartners. We know the First Amendment like we know the Pledge and our multiplication tables."

"The most important thing we've learned about our Constitution is that it protects our rights," Madelyn explained to the adults in the room. "It doesn't give us rights—those are given to us at birth—but it protects those rights and it protects those rights for everyone, even for those who are very different from us and have very different opinions from us. That's what America is all about."

"We also vote for student government officers and representatives," said Pooja, her mother nervously scrutinizing every syllable. "When they campaign they cannot say anything about another candidate—we wish everyone running for office in this country had to follow that rule. They tell what they stand for and make a speech that is broadcast to our whole student body. We all go to the polls to vote and everyone learns how to be a respectful winner and a respectful loser." Pooja and the others held up election posters. Each looked similar to the others. "These are some of the posters from our last election," she explained. "Everyone has a poster made the same way so that the amount of money that a person has isn't part of the campaign."

By this point, the packed ballroom was rapt. The parents had started to relax, confident their children were up to the challenge. Mary looked on proudly. And the students continued to offer their elementary-aged civics lesson, holding up election posters, copies of kindergarten constitutions, and signs like "We Make Voting Fun" or "We Honor Differences."

"We vote in our classrooms too," Will shouted, fidgeting with his small glasses. "We practice voting a lot so that we will develop good habits for living in a democracy and so that we will do it for all of our lives. We vote for our class representatives for student government and for the recycling program. We do quick votes for things like what cookie we will get for lunch one week and for the movie the PTA will show on family movie night. Our kindergartners cast their ballots for which face they will carve on their Halloween pumpkin. And we all learn that it is important for everyone to be a part of decision making."

As the students' time on the stage neared its conclusion, they went into their final piece. "We also practiced democracy by having a student Constitution," Josh explained, his young voice powerfully amplified by the mike. "We wrote the Constitution last year. First we wrote our preamble, and we will say it for you.

We the students of Nursery Road, in order to form a more perfect school, establish fairness, ensure peace for everyone, provide for common safety, promote equality for all students, secure the blessings of freedom for ourselves and the future of our school, and do ordain and establish this Constitution for the students of Nursery Road Elementary School

"Every homeroom ratified the new Constitution and we had an assembly for the signing. All the signers even had special engraved pens. Our original Constitution is framed and every homeroom has a copy."

The group concluded with a song about the Constitution. While the children sang, their bodies freely moved with the music. Miller exhorted the more recalcitrant adults in the audience to join him:

> The U.S.A. was just starting out
> A whole brand-new country.
> And so our people spelled it out
> They wanted a land of liberty.
> And the Preamble goes like this:
> We the people,
> In order to form a more perfect union,
> Establish justice, insure domestic tranquility,
> Provide for the common defense,
> Promote the general welfare and
> Secure the blessings of liberty
> To ourselves and our posterity
> Do ordain and establish this Constitution for the United States of America.

A five-minute standing ovation followed. The students were not present for most of it—as soon as they finished, they rushed off the stage; Will and Miller had a tic-tac-toe game that needed finishing, and the others were eager to start sightseeing with their families.

For the adults, however, the moment lingered. "I didn't know children this young could speak with such eloquence and firsthand familiarity about our founding principles," commented one legislator from South Dakota. When the stars emerged outside the hall with their families, the legislator approached them, the eyes behind his glasses as electric with excitement as young Will's. "I'm a former teacher," he said, "and I just want you guys to know that you were the best thing all week at this conference, and the first thing I'm going to do when I go home is urge my colleagues to join me in doing everything we can to ensure that every school in our state becomes a First Amendment School."

❧

Two years after the students' presentation in Seattle, a lot had changed at Nursery Road. Although some of the national attention remained, much of the

staff had moved on, including several of the project's most staunch supporters. The children who'd participated in the school's first student government
had all moved on to middle school. And perhaps most significant, Christina
Melton had replaced Mary Kennerly as principal.

Melton, attractive, dark-haired, and young, first discovered she wanted to
be an educator in the third grade, thanks to her teacher, Ms. Libby Baker.
"From that point on," she explained one afternoon in August 2007, "I've had
it mapped out completely—and I've followed it ever since."

Melton came to NRES from a rural county, where she went from classroom
teacher to curricular planner to assistant principal to principal. She described
her philosophy of leadership this way: "All stakeholders must be empowered
to make good decisions that are good for children, first and foremost."

To that end, Melton had spent the summer before her first year at the school
speaking with staff and asking them three questions:

1. Tell me about the school.
2. Tell me what I need to look closely at to improve the school.
3. Tell me what I need to do to make you more successful at your work.

Every staff member came in for an individual meeting to discuss the
questions. It was during these conversations, Melton explained, that a lot
of patterns emerged. "Clearly, the strength of the school is in its history, its
traditions, and its commitment to parental involvement. That was encouraging to me, because my leadership philosophy is grounded in having the entire
faculty involved and then debriefing what we're doing, why we're doing it,
and creating a more reflective community—so that everyone has a voice and
it isn't just a few people.

"Too often in education we feel like we're doing the right thing. But do we
know we're doing the right thing? That's why I want my faculty to develop a
deep knowledge of one thing, not a surface knowledge of many things."

To follow through on that vision, Melton asked every teacher to choose the
three most important areas of their own personal growth. Then, she promised
that time would be allocated on the second and fourth Thursdays of every
month for teachers to build their knowledge base in these areas. "Oftentimes,
teachers have too much on their plate," said Melton, "so I'm trying to sim-
plify things so they can go deeper into their professional practice. I follow the
rule of the Three P's—PLAN, PRIORITIZE, PURSUE."

As I spent the next few days speaking with members of the community
about the school, I found that people were eager to speak about the transition.
As one teacher put it, "Different people have different points of focus. I do
think leadership has many different sides. There are leaders who give people

voices and those who don't; there are leaders who don't have agendas and there are those who have agendas but say they don't."

I asked the teacher to elaborate. "The First Amendment is not a project-checklist-show, it's a belief system. And so although this school may not be labeled a First Amendment School anymore, this school is still very much run democratically—the voices are being heard. In fact, they're being heard more now than they were before. Several aspects of the school were in disrepair. I guess I see now that you can't shove a belief down people's throats—you have to let them have a voice."

Later that day two other teachers—both younger, newer members of the faculty—shared similar stories. "We're more focused now," said a cheerful blonde woman named Sharon. "We have a better idea of where we're going. You can't give every comment equal value—you have to have a leader who keeps the group on point. I think Mary wanted to value everyone's opinion, but maybe she did it a little too much. Christina's consistency has had a calming effect. It's very clear she remembered what we told her over the summer." Sharon's teaching partner, Emily, added her belief that "Christina acts; last year it was more talk."

"Initially," Sharon said, "the change in leadership was very hard for our staff because we were all used to things being done a certain way. I think Mary assumed the staff was willing to do certain things, and she tailored her actions accordingly. She got the idea people just wanted her to make a decision—I don't think she really understood how much the faculty wanted a voice. For example, she created a 'vision team' last year and made it open to everyone, but most of the people who went were the newest people. That told me everyone else was disillusioned by that point.

"A year ago, I'm not sure everyone would have known what the school's primary focus was, because there were so many. This year, you ask anyone and you'll hear the same answer—we are champions of children. That clarity has made what we were already doing more explicit and helped people stay focused on our main task, which is helping children learn."

"Over time," Emily added, "I think we started *doing* stuff blindly. FAS turned into a program—and *doing things*. It became less of a foundation for the work itself. And so as new people came in, they took it for granted that other people would know why it was important. But just because you knew the 'why' at one point doesn't mean you'll keep knowing it."

Julius Scott, a quiet young assistant principal, agreed. "There is a greater sense of trust among the staff now. Mary was solid on the FAS stuff—but over time, it came to be associated too much with just her. She maintained the school's focus on it, but I don't know that it was an accurate indication of how people felt. I think it's essential that work like this be defined as a philosophy and not a program. This is about human development—and it should be framed as such."

Another teacher, one of the first I'd met at Nursery Road, thought back to those earliest days. "At first," she said, "we as a faculty were so excited. But we weren't able to be really honest—it became a dictatorship—we did great things for the kids but it was the complete opposite with the adults. We've been put more in charge now. Mary gave us choices, but a lot of the time going against the grain was more trouble than it was worth. I don't think any principal should be at the same school for twenty-three years; she lost touch over the years. FAS was a way for her to feel good again. She felt excited about something. And yet as she felt like she was losing control, she exerted more of it, and a feedback loop started. The work became a 'to do' list, and there was very little dialogue. As a result, the quality of instruction went down, and it turned into a colony of islands."

My last visit was to the class of Lynne Riddick, a twenty-six-year veteran of the school and a fifth-grade social studies teacher. "The FAS project sort of came upon us five years ago. We didn't realize what we were into. I think that was a mistake; before a big new project starts, everyone should know what they're getting into. Historically, we're so excited by new stuff we tend to go too big too soon too fast. I think it makes more sense to keep it small.

"I also think we were doing too many things at one time. There was an aspect of the dog and pony show to some of it, which came with a cost. At the same time, our children learned immeasurably from those experiences— they'll remember what they did forever."

I asked Lynne, a master teacher whose facial expressions switch easily between stern and joyful, to imagine she could travel back through time in order to identify some key moments where she might urge the school to do things differently. Her answer was instantaneous. "The first stop I'd make is back to the first time the project was announced to the faculty. I'd urge people to ask more questions—people needed to have a clearer sense of what they were signing up for; otherwise, what you get is a small group of dedicated soldiers, but over time that can breed resentment. Everyone needed to have the experience of direct involvement. But it ended up being a small group of people."

As Lynne and I spoke, her next class of students started settling into their seats, their ten-year-old manic energy soothed and directed by their teacher's authoritative calm and support. "I think it's important for leaders to make sure they're not focusing too much on adult activities—the things we do with our children must be age-appropriate, and that's why some of the stuff we did didn't work very well. In my mind, our student council was a flop—the kids that were involved did great work, but it didn't carry over to the larger student body. By contrast, morning meeting is the best thing we've done. I wonder if that's better—let them be leaders in their *classrooms*, not the school. They thrive on that positivity, and we're teaching them about community in a way that's age-appropriate.

"In retrospect, a lot of time we would go through processes but people felt as though the decisions were already made. That doesn't make someone want to participate the next time. I think part of the problem is that when you get to a position of power it's easy to fall out of touch with what's happening in the trenches. But the bottom line is adults want their opinion to be valued, just like the kids do. So if I had to give the last five years a single headline, it would be that while we bungled some of the adult work, we learned to listen to children in a deeper way—we helped them discover their voices."

The bell rang and Ms. Riddick's morning meeting began. As the students sat in a circle, everyone was given an opportunity to share anything on their mind—this is done regularly to help everyone learn more about each other and also to surface ideas that could distract children if they aren't allowed to express them. A young boy volunteered that his family's Alpaca was giving birth. Lynne asked if the other children had questions. I watch as the boy—shy, slender, uncertain—grows in confidence as scores of hands go up, eager to learn more about this exciting development.

❧

On my last day in town, I meet up with Mary to get her sense of what took place. Now working in the district office as a social studies curriculum coordinator, Mary didn't learn that her old job was being advertised in the local newspaper until late one Friday afternoon. Because the faculty had already left for the weekend, Mary frantically tracked down each teacher by phone so no one would be as surprised as she was to learn of the coming change.

As we settle into a table at a Panera Bread Company, Mary looks disappointed and hurt, but also resilient. Together, we reflect on the ways in which the school did and did not reach its goal of becoming a fully developed democratic learning community. Mary quickly identifies two constraints: "Time, on one hand, and the people who didn't have a passion for the work, on the other. Unless I kept the fires going, people wouldn't always follow through. The hardest issue was having a good governance structure—a way for people to be highly involved in decision-making so that decisions were truly reflective of consensus.

"How do you find the time to repeatedly bring those people together and let them really reflect on what needs to be done? I heard a lot of people asking for input, but then those same people wouldn't come to meetings. I just couldn't figure out how to fully engage everyone.

"That was the message I don't think I ever fully got across—that every person's voice needs to be heard. I think for schools to be really effective, adults must have that time to reflect together on what needs to be done, and who will do it, and how. Things move at such a fast pace that frequently you lose the time to bring people together.

"Still, when I look back I am most proud of the many opportunities we provided for our children to experience democracy in both small and large ways. In the process, I think our adults also learned about how to be a part of democracy, and how to set up an environment that helps children do that."

As I get up to leave, Mary hands me a favorite artifact of hers—the school's first kindergarten constitution.

> We promise to help each other play and learn
> If someone falls we will help them up
> We will care about each other and share
> We will not tattle tell or fight
> We will be friends even when no one is watching
> And not laugh at each other's mistakes
> We will say "good try"
> And we will not break our promises.

Chapter Eight

Monadnock Community Connections School (Swanzey, New Hampshire)

Several members of MC²'s community, including Director Kim Carter (center), meet to discuss school improvement strategies.

As the lights dim and photographs begin to appear on the large screen behind her, nineteen-year-old Cass Carland steadies herself against the podium with alabaster hands, takes a sip of water, and looks out at the crowd in front of her.

"My sophomore year of high school I was given an old all-manual camera," she says, her calm voice amplified by the microphone attached to her black t-shirt. "It was suggested that I photograph the same thing over and over again trying different combinations of aperture and shutter speed. My school was at a farm at the time, and I spent hours wandering around snapping shot after shot of rotting logs covered with mushrooms, purple anemones, butterflies on yarrow, and tractors in the mud. Unable to detach the camera from my eye, I photographed chess games and typing hands and little kids picking their noses. Most of the pictures came out blurry or unexposed, but I felt I was onto something."

The pictures behind Cass do not correspond to her narration. They are neither blurry nor unexposed, and there is not a butterfly in the bunch. Instead the images are of people—mostly young—in various stages of action, inaction, laughter, boredom, anxiety. "Around this time I discovered a reason to keep taking pictures," she explains. "As with a great many passions and obsessions, it had root in a secret fear I carried around with me constantly. It was the fear of losing, the fear of forgetting. The thought that every moment was slipping away—carrying me from the things I loved—made me fear the future, and made me cling to the past in a way that held me back. I feared change."

It is May 29, 2007, and Cass is in the midst of her graduation gateway, a required rite of passage for all students of Monadnock Community Connections School, or MC² for short. Cass's descriptions of her photographs make up one part of the forty-five-minute public presentation that will be assessed to determine her readiness for the adult world. "I'm a Phase Four student at MC² (see figure 8.1)," Cass wrote in her letter of invitation to attend the gateway. "Phases here are the equivalent of grades. So Phase Four is the equivalent of being a senior. After each phase, the student needs to do a Gateway exhibition before moving on to the next phase. This will be my final exhibition to graduate. The exhibition will demonstrate my growth in understanding about myself as a learner and my relationship to the greater community."

As the audience of friends, family members, local officials, and national experts study the faces behind her, Cass provides some context to the images. "When you're a teenager, it's almost inevitable that you'll be self-absorbed. So you create a little world for yourself, that world of teenage intrigue; it's made up of your fellow cronies, a school building, laughter, a skate park, a backyard, affection, a junk car lot, a street at night, a cluttered bedroom, aggression, a park bench, a basement, a pool table—all things intense and

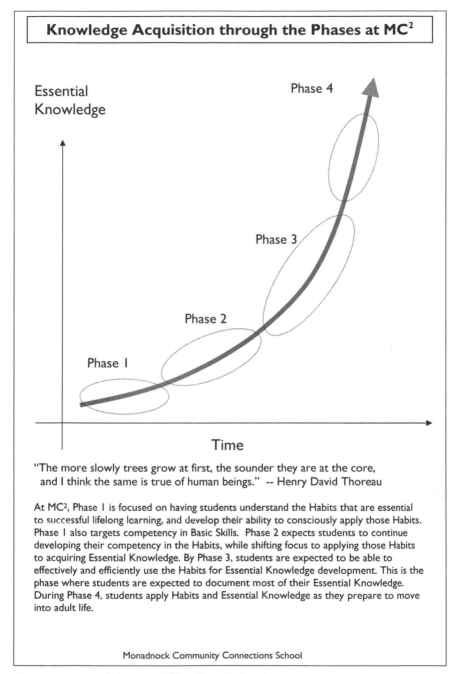

Figure 8.1. Knowledge acquisition through the phases at MC².

insecure. Things that seem so important at the moment, and don't seem to matter just a few years later. So it makes sense that I'd want to photograph it. As Bill Brandt said, 'it is part of a photographer's job to see more intensely than most people do.'"

Five years earlier, MC² was founded to help young people like Cass learn how to see more intensely. "I first heard about MC² from a friend who was planning to attend there the autumn it started," Cass recalls in her autobiography — another of the school's requirements for graduation. "I was weeding a garden, and as the sun blistered my neck and I planted delphiniums he wove a tale of a small student body and personalized education. To me it sounded like hope.

"I remembered the school again, a couple months later, when I was hiding in a classroom during lunch, one week into my sophomore year at Keene High. It meant leaving everything I knew, but as the bell rang and I felt a clutter of panic send me into fight-or-flight mode, I knew it probably wouldn't be worse. As I meandered the halls looking for my math class, late, and watched some kid get slammed into his locker, I wondered if there was any school where I could let my guard down. The 'No Harassment Policy' was nothing but a piece of paper, I knew from experience. Mostly, I knew I needed a change."

MC² was launched after an intensive visioning process that brought together diverse members of the Monadnock Regional School District, a collaborative district made up of eight semirural and rural towns in the southwestern part of New Hampshire. More than 160 people participated in the meetings. Participants broke into smaller groups and spent time brainstorming their ideas of what education in the ensuing century would need to look like to give young people what they needed.

After making sense of the data, the group's ideas clustered around four characteristics for a quality education:

1. There must be a lower student-to-teacher ratio, so instruction can be personalized.
2. There must be smaller schools, so interpersonal relationships can have a greater likelihood to flourish.
3. There must be a commitment to personalization, so that an individualized education can be guaranteed to every student.
4. There must be opportunities to learn that extend beyond the school's walls, so that students can gain valuable experiences that help them identify their greatest areas of interest and passion.

Kim Carter, a lifelong educator and former New Hampshire Teacher of the Year, took this shared vision and used it to design MC² as a public school of choice for students in search of a different learning experience than the traditional high school. "I feel like this place is the island of the misfit toys," Carter first explained to me, one fall afternoon a few years after the school first opened. "Most of our children bring with them painful stories of not fitting in, or of struggling academically. But here, they belong. That's why I feel like personally I'm seeing thirty years of my work coming to a confluence."

At the time, MC² was tucked away in a labyrinth of Antioch University's administration buildings. Initially, as Cass referenced in her gateway, the school was housed in a building on a local farm. (It opened with twenty-seven students.) In a year, it would need to move again, reflecting the fragility of its role in the community and the omnipresent challenges Kim faced in keeping the school afloat. "Our plan was to add twenty-five students a year until we reached 100," she said, "but over the years we have experienced the enrollment fluctuations that are characteristic of a fledgling school. And we continue to have our challenges."

In the autumn of 2004, as the school's then-forty-five students shuffled between a central multipurpose room and two adjoining classrooms, Kim, a forty-something mother of three with wavy brown hair and deeply set blue-gray eyes that radiate intelligence from behind her glasses, explained how the school took the community's shared vision and fashioned it into an actionable structure for a school. "All learning at MC² is *personalized*," she said, "which means the work that takes place here is tailored to each student's personal learning needs. It's *experiential*, which means our students learn by doing. It's *negotiated*, which means our students participate in decisions about what they will learn, and it's *community based*, which means much of the learning takes place through a variety of community interactions."

A thoughtful young teacher named Elizabeth Cardine jumped in to outline how the school's four points of emphasis are used to form a comprehensive curriculum. "At MC², each student works with a faculty advisor to develop an individualized learning plan, or ILP (see textbox 8.1). In the ILPs, our students are asked to set learning goals for themselves, based on our schoolwide Learner Expectations, which have five central components":

1. *Basic Skills*, such as reading, writing, mathematics, listening, and speaking, etc.
2. *MC² Habits*, of which there are three: being self-directed, owning a commitment to lifelong learning, and acting like a responsible member of the community.

3. *Habits of Mind*, which are: problem-solving, decision-making, critical and creative thinking, communication, organization, leadership, management, and the effective use of information and technology.
4. *Habits of Being*, which are: work ethic, quality work, ethical character, curiosity and wonder, and collaboration. And
5. *Essential Knowledge*, which is grounded in the following disciplines: English/Language Arts, Math, Science, Social Studies, the Arts, Foreign Languages, and Technology.

Text box 8.1

Individualized Learning Plan (ILP) Process

- Student takes "Learning Style Preference Survey" in advisory to determine learning style preference
- Discuss the meaning of the "Learning Style Preference Survey" with Advisor
- Identify strengths, and areas where the student most needs to growth
- Brainstorm interests student wants to incorporate into his or her learning
- Identify the goals student has and/or goals from learning team (parents, advisor, exhibition panelists) recommendations
- Select three potential Internship focuses
- Incorporate feedback from advisor, parents
- Identify the learning standards student will focus on: MC^2 Habits, Habits of Mind, Habits of Being, Basic Skills, and Essential Knowledge ILP goals will be used in determining schedule choices

---

"To bring these skills and habits to bear," she continued, "we have detailed rubrics for each of the core habits. In this era of testing, people like to say attributes like curiosity are important, but there's no way to measure it, so it really doesn't have a place in the modern school. Well, we've figured out how to quantitatively measure a qualitative attribute like curiosity (see figure 8.2), and, most importantly, we're helping our students develop clarity around what such an attribute looks and sounds like."

❧

It's true. The rubrics—each with five descriptive cells (novice, advanced beginner, competent, proficient, and expert)—clarify the school's values and

Habits of Being	**Curiosity & Wonder**				Fall 2004 √
	Light = Job Shadow Expectations Mid = Internship Expectations Dark = Apprenticeship Expectations				
	Novice	**Advanced Beginner**	**Competent**	**Proficient**	**Expert**
Value of Knowledge	Is uninterested in new things; is bored in and out of school	Is interested in ideas in one or a few areas; is bored by things outside of his/her own interests	Loves learning in one or a few areas; can find some interest in other areas	Finds interest in many different areas	Values knowledge for its own sake; loves learning new things; finds interest in everything
Question Making	Does not ask or form questions	Can use other people's questions to seek answers but does not form or ask his/her own questions	Uses other people's questions and forms his/her own questions in school	Forms new and original questions in school; begins to form questions outside of school	Constantly considers new and original questions about the world around him/her; actively seeks answers
Openness to New Ideas	Dismisses ideas that are unfamiliar or that contradict student's own experiences	Is open to some unfamiliar or contradictory ideas	Considers unfamiliar or contradictory ideas with an open mind	Considers unfamiliar or contradictory ideas with an open mind; compares and contrasts different viewpoints	Seeks out and explores new and contradictory ideas
Connection Making	Does not see a connection between topics	Begins to see connections between topics	Sees connections between topics	Sees connections between topics and begins to make connections to own life	Sees and looks for connections between topics; can find a way to connect any topic to his/her own life
Comfort with Complexity	Shuts down when questions can't be answered easily	Attempts to work through complex ideas, but gets frustrated easily	May get frustrated by complexity, but does not give up completely	Is comfortable with a complex challenge	Is inspired and excited by unanswered questions and complexity

Figure 8.2.   One of the MC²'s evaluative rubrics. The school's curriculum is aligned around seventeen aspirational habits of heart and mind.

shared purpose. Students are constantly asked to assess their strengths and weaknesses and to choose behavioral goals. Teachers chart student progress for each habit via an online assessment tool that places student behavior along a nonlinear continuum. (The school uses a program called FirstClass to create a private online network accessible to teachers, students, and parents.) "All of this information is available for viewing at anytime by the students, their parents, or our faculty," Kim adds excitedly, "so that anyone can view a student's progress on a particular goal in 'real time.'"

This organizational clarity extends across the school's four main types of learning opportunities: internships (one-on-one relationships with an adult mentor outside the school building), challenges (activities designed to promote critical thinking, collaboration, and self-reflection), skill development (focused attention on essential knowledge), and treks (field experiences that allow students to develop skills and apply their learning in a meaningful setting).

The last type of learning opportunity—treks—has been particularly powerful for many of MC²'s young people. Students receive their own *Wilderness Orientation Trek Journal*. On the front cover, the student must sign his or her name above the school's mission statement: "Empowering each individual with the knowledge and skills to use his or her unique voice effectively, and with integrity, in co-creating our common public world." Inside, the journal's first page explains that the trek is designed "to prepare you to become a successful member of the MC^2 community." Five types of expectations are introduced and explained: physical ("pull your own weight and push yourselves past preconceived limits"); emotional ("trust and be open to others, and be respectful to yourself"); social ("work productively and cooperatively with compassion"); intellectual ("learn about yourself; your strengths and struggles"); and spiritual ("develop an awareness of how you fit into the big picture").

What follows is all the information they'll need on the trek—which takes place each August—from hiking to foot care to basic astronomy. Each blank page is seeded with a thought-provoking idea. One page quotes Martin Luther King Jr.: "The ultimate measure of a man is not where he stands in moments of comfort and convenience, yet where he stands at times of challenge and controversy." Another cites Yoda: "Do or do not; there is no try."

One fall day in 2005, in a spare white conference room with gray carpeting, a single table, and eight chairs, five MC^2 students practice the presentations they will make the following night to the school community. Although two months have passed since their treks took place, the students have been working steadily to perfect their ten-minute talks, which are supposed to reflect what they learned, both individually and as a member of the group, during the trek. No one is considered a complete member of the MC^2 community until he or she delivers an acceptable presentation, so there is a palpable seriousness and energy to their work.

One student, a young girl named Tawnya ("but everyone calls me 'Tabby'") shares a thoughtful set of slides and reflections on her relationships with the other students on the trek. "I want to be a student at MC^2 because everyone is so supported here," she concludes. "I really felt that on the trek and it gave me a lot of perspective about myself." Tabby is followed by a slim early teen named Sam. Wearing a green t-shirt and glasses, Sam rocks back and forth as he speaks, occasionally touching his shaved head gently. One immediately senses his vulnerability; it's easy to imagine him being preyed on at a typical public school. He confirms the worry during his presentation: "My last experience of school was . . . it was . . . horrible," he whispers, "but I like this place because it's small and you can vote on things and stuff."

MC^2 is small, although its students do cover a spectrum of socioeconomic backgrounds and call a host of different towns in southern New Hampshire home. Many of those students have stories similar to Sam's and Cass's; the traditional public school experience left them feeling forgotten, threatened, and invisible. MC^2 is the place where they have discovered, as the school's mission promises, their "unique voice" and how to use it effectively.

WHAT ARE PERFORMANCE-BASED ASSESSMENTS?

Performance assessments are tools that allow teachers to gather information about what students can actually do with what they are learning – science experiments that students design, carry out, analyze, and summarize; computer programs that students create, test, and refine; persuasive essays that students write; research inquiries they pursue, seeking and assembling evidence about a question, and presenting it in written and oral form. Whether the skill or standard being measured is writing, speaking, mathematical literacy, or research, students actually perform tasks involving these skills while the teacher observes, gathers information, then scores the performance based upon a set of pre-determined criteria.

These assessments typically consist of three parts; a task, a scoring guide or rubric, and a set of administration guidelines. The development, administration, and scoring of these tasks requires teacher development to ensure quality and consistency. Research suggests that such assessments are better tools for showing the extent to which students have developed higher order thinking skills, such as the abilities to analyze, synthesize, and evaluate information. They lead to more student engagement in learning and stronger performance on the kinds of authentic tasks that better resemble what they will need to do in the world outside of school. They also provide richer feedback to teachers, leading to improved learning outcomes for students.

One Halloween day a few years ago, the school's commitment to honoring all voices was gently challenged when a group of parents and students assembled in one of the small school's few rooms to discuss a new dress code policy. According to Kim, a voracious reader equally likely to quote developmental psychologists, historians, or the fictional characters of the tv show *Scrubs*, discussing the issue provided "a perfect opportunity to have students be the subjects of their own education, as opposed to objects who have school done to them. It was a way to have them use the dialogue skills they have been developing to look at a policy that supposedly took their concerns into account."

It was also, she added, a way to solicit parent involvement. "Family involvement is a cornerstone of our program," she said proudly. "Parents are valued as the individuals who know their children best and are integrally involved in the creation and monitoring of their children's learning plans, the assessment of student progress and achievement, and the development of our shared culture and community. To communicate how deeply we believe this, we ask parents to sign the admissions agreement and submit an essay during the application process in which they are asked to bring their expertise to the process of helping their child reach his or her fullest potential."

As the small group of teachers, students, and parents found seats around a conference table, each person was handed a copy of the proposed policy. "In order to maintain a professional atmosphere of learning, mutual respect, and safety," it read, "while allowing for freedom of expression, students and faculty will abide by the following code of dress."

1. Students and faculty will be allowed to wear clothes that do not distract from the learning process.
2. Students and faculty will be allowed to wear clothes that express themselves as long as they do not disrupt our environment of safety, respect and professionalism.
3. Student and faculty will wear clothes that conform to health code regulations (i.e. cleanliness, no bare feet, etc.)

Although a list of forbidden attire followed, the group was more interested that morning in clarifying what constitutes professionalism. "What does professionalism mean anyway, and why do we need to dress professionally?" asked one young girl in a red sweatshirt. "I want to be comfortable here." A particularly articulate student named Andy, dressed as a fireman to honor the holiday, got even more specific. "I think this professionalism thing is really a catch-all that's being used by the faculty to get rid of fashion trends they don't like, like girls showing their midriffs." A wizard, a policeman, and Abraham Lincoln, also seated around the table, nodded in affirmation.

The dress code conversation was possible, Kim explained, because the community had already spent the previous two years developing its formal governance structure (see figure 8.3). Ten people—Kim, a parent, a teacher, and seven students—met weekly to put forth a plan of action they could eventually present to the full community. Along the way, students took the lead investigating other governance models and structures, attending conferences, and contacting other schools that shared MC²'s commitment to consensus and youth voice.

In time, the group agreed that the school would be governed by three branches—executive, legislative, and judicial. Once this was settled, the committee focused its attention on defining the legislative branch first. They decided that its anchor would be a governance council, on which students would always hold the majority of seats. The director, however, would also

EXECUTIVE BRANCH

Director of MC2,
representing MRSD School Board,
Superadvisory Union 38,
State Government, and
Federal Government.
The Director has veto power over the other branches.

LEGISLATIVE BRANCH

Staff Senate
This is the main forum for FACULTY VOICE in the policy making process.

Governance Council
This is the main forum for STUDENT VOICE in the policy making process.

Whole Community Meeting
This is the main forum for PARENT VOICE in the policy making process.

Community Meeting
This regularly scheduled time is for staff and students to address community concerns during school hours.

Open Session
This is a quarterly opportunity for any community member to express a concern and have it debated, not resolved.

Proposed Governance Structure
by the Governance Structure Committee
Approved Spring 2005
Empowering each individual with the knowledge and skills to use his or her unique voice effectively, and with integrity, in co-creating our common public world.

JUDICIAL BRANCH

Conflict Resolution
Through Peer Mediation (between peers) and Win-Wins (not necessarily between peers) issues get resolved.

Appeals and Recommendations Committee
Students and parents may appeal consequences.
Teachers request recommendations for consequences.
In process

Students In Action
Students help other students through structured support.
In process

Figure 8.3. A map of the MC²'s governance structure.

have a vote, and the parent representatives would be empowered to block any policy they strongly disagreed with. "This purposeful balance of voice and power," Kim shared, "forced everyone to practice the skills that now allow us to discuss, deliberate, debate, and have dialogue while staying in relationship with each other. These skills do not come naturally or easily. But we have found they are critical to democratic processes, especially when dealing with the issues that surface emotions and bring strongly held convictions into conflict. Learning to disagree without losing sight of each other's perspective and contribution, I now see, can't become a habit without a lot of practice."

Following the morning dress code conversation, several students entered one of the two classrooms to attend the Use It or Lose It class. Not surprisingly, MC² has an unconventional curriculum. The day is divided into three blocks. During the first block of that semester, students chose between Latin, Spanish, or Sign Language. Second block was either *Museum Studies* or *Use it or Lose It*. Third block offered four choices: Advertising, an interdisciplinary math and social studies class called Flatland (named after Edwin Abbott's book of the same title), a course called The Life of Birds (yes, The Life of Birds,) and a class called It's About Time.

Despite the atypical menu of choices, students are given clear indications of what they'll need to progress as a learner. In fact, a checklist of expectations outlines what must be accomplished in order to graduate.

The Use It or Lose It class, according to the school's list of courses, was designed to provide "a study of First Amendment principles and practice." On this particular day, a young teacher named Andrew was the teacher in charge. Almost immediately, students confronted him in subtle and not-so-subtle ways. Andrew—young, smart, and inexperienced—chose to avoid the challenges. As a result, students left the room at will throughout the period. One boy napped on two chairs in the back of the room. Another consistently jingled his keys.

Slowly, the group began reviewing some work the students had done on developing their own assessment rubrics. The class seemed disengaged, and Andrew seemed unprepared.

Then he decided to build on the students' prior knowledge by suggesting they create a rubric for determining how well someone exercises their freedom of speech. The students immediately responded to the new direction. "I think a novice is someone who either doesn't speak, or doesn't know what the First Amendment is," said one boy. "An advanced beginner believes he has the right to say whatever he wants to say," added another student, bedecked in motocross symbols. The group decided that a competent user of free speech would understand what it means but still feel cautious about using his voice publicly. A proficient user would know her rights but perhaps push inappropriately for their consideration. Finally, a girl named Amber suggested that an expert user "knows and uses their rights properly, attempts to explain those rights to others, and follows their conscience."

It was an impressive sea change for the group and a reminder of how skilled teachers must be if they are to strike the right balance between freedom and structure in a classroom setting. Once the rubric was completed, Andrew asked the students to use it in assessing themselves during the class. The narcoleptic boy in the back of the room perked up. "I'd rank myself as proficient," he said, "because I didn't speak but I was listening."

The next block provided some time to speak with the students of Public Achievement (www.publicachievement.org), a national public action program for youth in which students start different action groups based on interests, and adult coaches serve in a support capacity.

During our time with the group, however, the students were more interested in sharing stories about why they came to MC². Each story was similar—these were young people who felt they had escaped from somewhere else to find a safer home. One boy was publicly ridiculed as a "faggot" at a school-sponsored assembly. Another got picked on relentlessly. "I've always been intelligent," he said, "but after getting picked on for so long I started bashing heads. That's when I realized I needed to switch schools." A third boy, a senior named Kyle, spoke most directly about the difference in him since coming to MC²: "This school really helped me look at myself and say, 'I want to be different.'" A younger, smaller boy sitting very close to Kyle quickly added: "And I'm his protégé!"

While Kyle and the other students were sharing their story, Cass Carland was in her advertising class, an experience she chose to write about in her graduation portfolio. "I finally experienced the joy of learning for the sake of learning," Cass explained. "I was fascinated because the class combined two of my greatest interests—psychology and design. These classes were also good for my learning style.

At the end of each school day, every MC² student spends twenty minutes writing an end-of-day (EOD) report. As Kim explained, "For many of our families, MC²'s structures for family participation provide a supportive environment for them to be active partners in their child's learning. And the EOD is the foundational structure for this involvement."

More than a journaling exercise, the EODs give students a chance to develop their metacognitive skills by assessing their own progress, commenting on anything of significance for the day, and developing an electronic record of their experience at the school. Each EOD is automatically sent to the student's faculty advisor, parents, and Kim. The faculty advisors send nightly responses to the students and their parents.

"The EOD is a critical literary component," Kim adds. "Students are writing regularly, with feedback, for an immediate and specific purpose. And EODs form the basis for other requirements, such as documenting work and writing an autobiography. Finally, EODs also involve parents in students' literacy as they increase families' connection to MC² and to their children's progress." The utility of the exercise is not limited to students, either; teachers write their own EODs, which Kim reads and responds to weekly—an essential professional development step, she explained, since many of the school's teachers are so new to the classroom. To complete the circle, Kim writes her own weekly reflections—one for her staff and the other for the larger community.

Before leaving the school one day, Kim excitedly shared with a visitor some letters from MC² parents who she'd asked to write welcome notes to prospective families. "This is a good place to start fresh," one read. "Throw out any baggage from years gone by and enter this place with new and positive thoughts."

The comment reminded her of a student at the school, a young boy named Ricky, whose personal journey represents one of the school's most satisfactory successes. "When Ricky first arrived," Kim explains, "he came with a transcript of all F's. During the interview we asked him—as we ask all students—'What do you want to be?' 'I used to want to be a game warden,' he mumbled, 'but now my grades won't let me.' Some time has passed since then, and now he's really starting to find his voice and hold other kids accountable. In fact, we're really at the place where kids are making the changes in beautiful ways, and Ricky is now reaching kids who weren't being reached by the adults."

"Just the other day," Kim continued, her eyes encircled by smile wrinkles, "he went on a ride with a game warden, one where he got to spend some time on the job, and he came back yelling, 'I can be anything! I can be anything!'"

"When it comes to learning," Cass explained, her graduation gateway almost complete, "I've learned it's not about failure or success, it's not about being 'above average' or 'below average,' it's not about being better than everyone else. It's about discovering new things, about finding things to be passionate about; it's about putting yourself into unexplored territories. And learning is not supposed to be about making yourself better than someone else. That's why, I now see, our projects are supposed to have a community angle to them.

"I don't remember much of what I learned in middle and high school. There were so many facts presented to me; it was overwhelming. And it didn't matter if I really learned them; I only had to remember them long enough to take a test about it. I was depressed by the transitory nature of everything I did. All those papers I wrote were recycled, that African mask I made has long been rotting in a dumpster.

"But ask me about the world of advertising? Prepare yourself for a long dissertation on the insidious nature of promotion and the real agenda behind MTV. Or I can say what it's like to put on a photo show, or what photography really means to me. And if I'm asked what my spiritual beliefs are, I'd be able to show them from the Bible. I need information to be personally relevant, and something I'm passionate about—it can't be facts for the sake of head knowledge. It has to reach my heart.

"I can see different ways that my learning relates to the MC² mission statement: *Empowering each individual with the knowledge and skills to use his or her unique voice effectively, and with integrity, in co-creating our common public world.* What I've written in this portfolio so far is my own mission statement, especially my recognition of the importance of other people in my life. As long as I always hold fast to what I believe in a way that is honest, and use it effectively, everything for me will turn out OK."

Epilogue
Ways of Seeing
(Teec Nos Pos, Arizona)

*A solitary sign is posted along one of the Navajo Reservation's
many long-winding dirt roads.*

"You," says the pilot. "Please move forward. We need your body up here."

I'm aboard a "puddle jumper"—a Beech 1900D—about to leave Denver for the Four Corners airport in Farmington, New Mexico. The plane has two rows of single seats, eight to a side. There is no bathroom, no flight attendant, and—logic follows—no in-flight service. The boyish pilot gives us our basic instructions, including a brief shuffling of seat assignments to better distribute the weight throughout the aircraft. He then hops into the cockpit, into which we have an unimpeded view. "I just flew this route," he says, looking back, "and it gets pretty bumpy when we head over the mountains. My advice to you is to sit tight, strap that seatbelt on, and do your best to enjoy the ride."

Despite being the largest sovereign territory in the United States—covering nearly 27,000 square miles, including all of Northeastern Arizona and parts of New Mexico and Utah—the Navajo Reservation is difficult to reach. The closest major American cities—Albuquerque, Salt Lake City, Denver—are several hours away. Even our aerial trek to Farmington leaves my colleagues and me eighty miles short of the final destination, Red Mesa High School.

We begin our descent with no sign of the airport—just a flat terrain, infrequent treetops, long dirt roads, and a sprinkling of mobile homes, each scattered randomly across the land like Legos.

The plane finds a runway and drops us off at the front door of the tiny commuter airport in Farmington. Once inside, I see the headline for the local newspaper. It's October 2005, and although all the major papers are abuzz with the news of President George W. Bush's decision to nominate White House counsel Harriet Miers for the U.S. Supreme Court, the *Daily Times* leads with a local story: "Family Grieves for Local Soldier Killed in Iraq."

∽◈∾

The Navajo of the American Southwest speak dialects of a language called *Athapaskan.* Archaeological evidence indicates that descendents of the modern Navajo people did not live here in significant numbers until the sixteenth century. By the mid-1500s, however, the Athapaskans—an ethnic group that included both the Navajo and the Apache tribes—and the more established Pueblo had become vital trading partners. The Spanish first mention the Navajo as a distinct group in the early 1600s. The name, taken from the Tewa Pueblo, whose settlement preceded the Navajo, means "thieves." (Most names used to identify Native American tribes in English are epithets by which their enemies referred to them.) The Navajo refer to themselves as the *Diné,* or "The People."

To continue our journey to the high school, we turn right out of the airport and onto Apache Street. Still close to Farmington, an adult video store is visible up ahead under a giant billboard: "Jesus is Watching You." Other businesses line the sides of the two-lane highway: Wagon Wheel Pawn Shop. Valley Scrap Metal. Singleton's Mobile Homes. Burger King. Navajo Food Distribution Program.

After fifteen miles, the road stretches out straight ahead. There is nothing to see except telephone poles, an occasional house, and fields of sagebrush. In the distance, at the edge of the horizon, reddish-brown mesas, buttes, and mountains greet the edges of the sky.

An hour and a half later, we turn into the small complex of buildings that make up the school. On one side of the street, rows of one-story beige trailers form orderly lines; these structures provide temporary housing during the week for most of Red Mesa's teachers. On the other side of the street, a dozen or so gray houses provide a slightly fancier form of lodging.

Where is the school, we wonder? We see a large beige building in front of us, but there is no sign. The only door we find looks as though it has been locked for decades. We stumble around the corner hoping to find Lorie Norton, the media teacher and our primary host. Instead we find John, a forty-something teacher, wind-tanned and whiskered.

"You all looking for someone?"

"We are. Is this the high school?"

"It sure is—are you guys the Freedom people?"

John leads us to Lorie's room, which serves as a sort of media headquarters for the school. Filled with rows of computers and a newly formed TV recording studio, the room also houses the school's radio station—KRMH, The Station that Jams the Nation. Lorie and her daughter, Katrina, are waiting inside. "We were wondering if you'd ever find us," says Lorie. Katrina, wearing black glasses, a black AC/DC shirt, black shorts, and dark purple eyeliner, is more to the point. "If you find anything out here, you should be excited."

It's nighttime, so our work with the school won't begin until the next morning. Lorie and Katrina lead us to our lodging—half a trailer for me, and a small gray house for my two colleagues, Molly and Emily. Outside the house is a giant shovel. "The wind blows so much at night, you may need to dig yourself out in the morning," Lorie warns. My teeth crunch on the grit and sand. We look up before separating; a sky full of stars glitters brilliantly above.

The next morning, we cross the street separating our temporary quarters from the school's main building. It's still early, but a steady stream of school buses has been pulling up in front of the school for at least an hour. Twenty-eight school buses serve Red Mesa's 900 or so elementary and high school students, many of whom live several hours away on unpaved, remote, rocky roads.

Red Mesa's principal, Tim Benally, is waiting for us in his office. Forty-four years old and the father of four, Tim has been the principal at Red Mesa for four years. He speaks with a Navajo "accent"—a slower, breathier cadence than my own, with extended emphasis placed on particular words. His eyes flicker with energy behind his spectacles. His skin is deeply tanned and healthy looking. He greets us with a giant smile and gives us a seat. "Do you feel lost?" he asks supportively. I nod. "That's what used to happen when I would go to the East Coast. I could only see this way," he explained, pointing straight up and down, "but I needed to see thiiis *way* (pointing straight out to either side). Which way was eaaast, which way was weeest," he whispers, smiling.

We ask Tim to describe his ideal outcomes, both for our visit and for his school in general. "In my lifetime," he says, "I know a Navajo will never be president. But I want our children to know that the power lies in their freedom to express themselves. There is some deep resentment here over what has happened over the years. There are two mindsets. One is about getting serious about education; in fact, one of the main dreams for people around here is to see their children graduate. That's always the biggest day of the year. I know it looks like there's no one here, but on that day you see the closest thing to a traffic jam we ever have.

"The other mindset is about reservation pride. A lot of the elders around here want parents to divert from the system and reconnect to their culture. Those mixed messages rub off on our kids, who can alternate between feeling motivated and not feeling motivated. I want them to feel enthusiastic about using their First Amendment freedoms to have a memorable time in high school, and to prepare them better for their lives after they graduate; it shouldn't just be about sports."

The Navajo elders have good reason to doubt the intentions of the "system." When the federal government assumed full control of native education in 1871, the first schools were charged with removing all traces of their students' indigenous cultures and replacing them with more "American ways" of thinking and living. As former Amherst president Merrill Gates outlined in an 1896 address:

> We have, to begin with, the absolute need to awakening in the savage Indian broader desires and ampler wants. To bring him out of savagery into citizenship we must make the Indian more intelligently selfish before we can make him unselfishly intelligent. We need to *awaken in him wants*. In his dull savagery he must be touched by the wings of the divine angel of discontent . . . Discontent with the teepee and the starving rations of the Indian camp in winter is needed to get the Indian out of the blanket and into trousers—and trousers with a pocket in them, and with a *pocket that aches to be filled with dollars!*

Although Gates was speaking a century ago, Indian boarding schools, funded by federal dollars, sought similar goals in the first few decades of the twentieth century. Students received "civilized" names and uniforms. Their hair was cut and their heads and bodies were washed with kerosene and lye. They were forbidden from speaking their own languages or practicing their own tribal religions. Inspections and drills took place daily. Platoons were organized according to age and rank. Scores of Christian missionary schools popped up across the country as well, charged with giving Indian children both the spiritual tools they would need for salvation and the social tools they would need to thrive in the United States.

Beginning in the 1930s, federal Indian education policy shifted again, leaving teachers freer to emphasize the role of Indian culture and language. But the legacy of the first schools, Tim explained, still lingers. "Most of our students can't speak their native language," he lamented. "They understand what their parents are saying, but they only respond in English. I'm hoping that in the same way the First Amendment belongs to all cultures and ideas, we can figure out a way to reconnect the students to a deeper sort of cultural belonging and appreciation. I don't want them to feel they need to choose between being an American and being an Indian. How I'm going to make that happen, I don't know. But I know that I want to."

We leave Tim's office to take our first tour of the school. It is a small, stout building. The walls above the lockers are painted in traditional Navajo patterns and colors, dressing up otherwise nondescript hallways. Low ceilings make the halls feel smaller than they are. Signs are written in English and Navajo.

We walk a short distance from the main building, separated by a common courtyard in which several boys play a wind-challenged game of basketball, to the cafeteria and gymnasium. The district's seal—an amalgam of American and Navajo images—frames the side of the gym that's facing us. When we notice it, Tim's smile widens. "We just had our first real First Amendment success thanks to that," he announces. The district planned to paint the seal on the center of the school's indoor basketball court. Students were adamant it be the school's mascot—the Redskins. After compiling a list of names on a petition and stating their case, the students got their wish. "That happened without any provocation by the adults," Tim adds. "So we know their interest is there."

Tim asks us to talk to every English class about the principles behind the First Amendment. His hope is that after we leave, the faculty can build on their students' shared sense of awareness and understanding. Molly, Emily, and I are led in different directions. We spend the next seventy minutes working with different classes, a ritual we will repeat five more times before heading home.

Each classroom has between fifteen and twenty-five students, whose ages range from thirteen to eighteen. In several classes, the students—mostly dressed in shades of black, blue, or gray—are asked to write down a question they'd like us to answer. Most questions feel forced and disconnected from any real point of interest. We are unknown quantities, and who really has a question about the First Amendment on a Tuesday morning, especially if you got up at 4:00 A.M. to catch the bus to school?

One question repeats itself across several classrooms, and it does sound like a point of real interest: "What is your culture?" I'm struck by this question, both in terms of how important it is to Red Mesa's students and how unprepared I feel I am to answer it.

Independently, we lead our classes through a discussion of the civic principles people must understand if a free society is to honor First Amendment freedoms for all people — individual rights, civic responsibilities (to guard the rights of others), and a commitment to debate differences with mutual respect. We notice how institutionalized the third "R" is at Red Mesa. Respect is simply a part of the culture. One teacher confesses she worries it sometimes makes the students too passive. "We're a protest without a cause," she says. This dynamic also makes it difficult to engage the students in an open discussion about such an abstract set of concepts.

Another teacher comments on this point later: "Our kids have a lot of cultural shyness," he says, "so they're not always sure how and when to enter a conversation." Later, as we eat seasoned beef and corndogs in the cafeteria, we agree this will be one of the unique challenges at a school like Red Mesa. "Asking kids to behave differently than their parents is very tricky," Molly says. "It can put them in a very uncomfortable situation. Perhaps our challenge is this: How can Red Mesa allow its kids to honor their families and still think deeply about the issues that matter to them?"

The workday concludes with a faculty meeting in the library. The room is long and rectangular, so the school's forty-six faculty members fan out across a series of individual desks and round tables, eating donuts and drinking Hawaiian Punch. The group is tired from the day.

After the meeting, we strike up a conversation with the two teachers closest to us. Kevin Martin, a tall man with a rigid posture and a workman's hands, speaks first. "I'm not sure how the idea of encouraging more freedom fits here at this school, but I do know a pervasive issue on this reservation has to do with the value of its natural minerals. If we can help ensure that more parents and kids are aware of the issues at stake and how to make their voices heard, then that's what I'd like to see."

Later, we learn more about the issues Kevin references. The Navajo's land contains some of the most valuable natural mineral deposits in North America — a fitting irony, since the land was initially given away because federal officials believed it to be worthless.

This bounty has had its cost. In 1922, outsiders first discovered the reservation land had something they wanted — oil. As major companies prepared their contracts, the Navajo — still operating under a decentralized system of local governments—lacked structured protocols that would allow them to reach agreement. The lack of a central body left the Navajo susceptible to the companies, which sought to cultivate relationships with different interest groups across the tribe. The Navajo formed a tribal council in 1923, but the real problems came several decades later, when in 1951 the key ingredient of nuclear weaponry—uranium—was discovered on the land.

Extractive companies moved in quickly, neglecting to tell their Navajo workmen about the dangers of the mineral they were mining. Workers returned home with uranium dust on their clothes. Piles of radioactive waste sat near people and animals. Some of the waste entered the water supply. It took years before tribal leaders made the connection between their people's health problems—and high incidences of certain types of cancer—and the mines. In 1990, Congress passed a law granting money to the people who had been hurt by uranium mining. But as Kevin pointed out, the issue was far from over.

Another teacher, an alert and sunny woman named Rebecca, shares a different obstacle. "People are afraid to speak up here," she says, "which is difficult for me as an outsider. You don't want to trespass and sound like a flaming radical—but you do want to help identify the correct channels and encourage the community to be more active."

Our visit culminates with a barbeque along the edge of the San Juan River. As the adults lay out plastic containers of homemade dishes across a picnic table, a young boy named Dylan Blackwater takes me to see cave drawings of the land's earliest human stewards. Alongside the still-colorful shapes of animals and hunters, drawn thousands of years ago, we see a modern addition: CUSTER DIED FOR YOUR SINS. Dylan takes my hand to lead me back to the group.

After dinner, I ask Rebecca, her ears and neck adorned with turquoise jewelry, to talk about her experiences as a non-Native teacher on the reservation. "I've been here thirteen years now," she begins, "so I obviously have found a way to make it work. It's lonely at times, but I just couldn't handle life in the city, and living here, every day allows me to walk in beauty."

I reflect on her comments on the short walk back from the car to my trailer that night. It is dusk, the wind is whipping around me, and the sky is a cosmic blue. Flashes of orange and magenta radiate from the tops of the mesas. I am alone. And I can see, thiiis *way*, to the eaaast and the weeest, for miles.

American Schools:
The Art of Creating a Democratic
Learning Community
Reflect. Connect. Create. Equip. Let Come.

Have questions or ideas about what you just read?
Join the online discussion of *American Schools* at
http://network.fivefreedoms.org.

Share your voice today!

Index

155

Monadnock Regional School District,
134
Morning Meeting (Kriete), 123

NASSP. *See* National Association of
Secondary School Principals
National Association of Secondary
School Principals (NASSP), 48
National Conference of State
Legislatures (NCSL), 123–25
National Paideia Center, 65, 103
National School Reform Faculty
(NSRF): CAC by, 25–28, *26*; Critical
Friendship by, 30; Facilitative
Leadership by, 30; leadership and,
30; Microlabs Protocol by, 77–79,
78; in schools, 25, 31, 32n12, 32n15,
65; Success Analysis Protocol by,
28, *29*
Native Americans, school for, 154–57.
See also Red Mesa High School
NCLB. *See* No Child Left Behind Act
NCSL. *See* National Conference of
State Legislatures
No Child Left Behind Act (NCLB):
accountability under, xii, 6, 41–42;
assessment under, xii, 6, 41–42;
focus of, xii; reauthorization of, xii;
resources under, xii; standardization
under, 41; student skills under, xii;
teaching practices for, xii, 41
NSRF. *See* National School Reform
Faculty
Nursery Road Elementary School:
Citizenship Day at, 116, 117;
community involvement at, 116,
117, 118–21, 126; curriculum
for, 121; democracy at, 115, 130;
disillusionment at, 127; FAS at,
117–18, 119–22, 127–28; Kennerly
at, 116–30; leadership at, 126–27;
"The Loss of the First Amendment"
by, 119, 121; Melton at, 126–29;
morning meeting at, 122–23, 129;
at NCSL, 123–25; NRES at, 121,

126; staff development at, 126; staff
engagement at, 129–30; student
Constitution for, 115, 124–25;
student government at, 117, 118,
124, 128–29

O'Connor, Sandra Day, xi–xiii
open space technology (OST), 94–95
Open Space Technology (Owen),
94–95
order *v.* control, 89
organizations: change within, 71–72, *72*;
for learning/teaching, xi, 22, 30, 31,
38–39, 47, 48, 49, 65, 66, 83, 97, 98,
143, 157
Origins of My Name, 25
OST. *See* open space technology
Our Courts web site, xiii
Owen, Harrison, 94–95

Padres Con Voz, 102–3, 107, 113
parents: attitudes/perceptions of, 73;
cocreation by, 56, 82; involvement
of, 38, 61, 79; key questions for, *61*,
73; reflection by, 17; school culture
and, 8–9, 10, 70, 73; SDP for, 61;
systems thinking by, 39–40, 46
Parent Teacher Association (PTA), 107,
113
Parks, Rosa, 7, 94
Pegasus Communications, 49
Pegasus Conference, 49
power: center of, 41; of civil friction,
93; as collective, 18; of individual,
9; leadership and, 72, 129; over
decision-making, 60–61, 65–66, 105,
129; relationships for, 45
principal, school: control by, 6–7;
explicit *v.* implicit goals by, 44–45;
personal vision of, 48, 59, 60; role
of, 47–48, 73, 82
Principles of Ecology (Capra), *57*
Project School, 24
Prologue, *3*
PTA. *See* Parent Teacher Association

About the Author

Sam Chaltain is the national director of the Forum for Education and Democracy, a DC-based education "action tank" devoted to restoring the public purpose of public education. He is also the founding director of the Five Freedoms Project, a national program that helps K–12 school communities create more democratic learning environments.

Previously, Sam spent five years at the First Amendment Center as the codirector of the First Amendment Schools program. He came to the Center from the public and private school systems of New York City, where he taught high school English and history. His first teaching experience was in Beijing, China, where he joined the faculty of the foreign languages department at Beijing Normal University as a visiting lecturer.

Sam's writings about public education have appeared in both magazines and newspapers, including *Education Week, USA Today*, and *The Huffington Post*, where he blogs regularly. He is the coauthor of two other books: *The First Amendment in Schools* (2003), and *First Freedoms: A Documentary History of First Amendment Rights in America* (2006).

Sam has a Master's degree in American studies from the College of William & Mary, and an M.B.A. from George Washington University, where he specialized in nonprofit management and organizational theory. He received his undergraduate degree from the University of Wisconsin at Madison, where he graduated with a double major in Afro-American studies and history.